I don't know much about ART - but I know a carbuncle when I see one...
Scarfe

SPACE ON EARTH

Architecture:
People and Buildings

CHARLES KNEVITT

THAMES METHUEN
LONDON
1985

For HJK and VMFK

Read not to contradict and confute; nor to believe and
take for granted; nor to find talk and discourse; but
to weigh and consider.
FRANCIS BACON

First published in Great Britain by Thames Television International Ltd,
149 Tottenham Court Road, London W1P 9LL

in association with Anglia Television and Channel Four Television.

Distributed by Methuen (Associated Book Publishers) Ltd,
11 New Fetter Lane, London EC4P 4EE.

Copyright © 1985 by Charles Knevitt and Anglia Television.

Phototypeset on a Linotron 202
in Century Old Style by
Stratatype, London NW1
and printed and bound by
Hollen Street Press, Slough.
Colour illustrations and cover printed by
Whitstable Litho, Whitstable, Kent.

Paperback ISBN 0 423 01440 4
Hardback ISBN 0 423 01430 7

CONTENTS

ACKNOWLEDGEMENTS

Many people contribute to a book such as this with little or no credit for all that they have put into it. This is an opportunity to correct that position to some extent.

Thanks are due to John Lloyd Fraser, producer and director of the Anglia Television series, for suggesting that I should write an accompanying book; to Ken Martin, the presenter, for sharing his thoughts, and Carolyn Schagen, the programme's researcher, for making available all the material she accumulated over two years.

Several of the passages in the book, particularly the chapter on architects, and numerous illustrations, first appeared in *The Times*. Colin Webb, deputy editor, and Colin Wilson, chief librarian, generously allowed their use here.

Nicholas Jones, my publisher and editor at Thames Methuen, was a great source of encouragement; with John Burke and John Lloyd Fraser, he suggested many clarifications and improvements. I would like to thank Deborah Pownall, the picture researcher, and Julia Brown, picture editor, for their tireless work chasing pictures from so many disparate sources. Thanks to Sue Ryall, the book's designer, for integrating text, pictures and quotations so effortlessly. And thanks to Nancy Young for preparing the index.

Ken Hayes, and his successor as editor of *Thames News*, Rob Kirk, allowed me days away from the bustle of the newsroom at Euston Road to compose my thoughts in the relative tranquillity of home.

Walter Ritchie lent his humanity and humour to a critique of the manuscript and saved me from embarrassing errors as well as making positive recommendations for improvements.

Sara Drake, my agent at A. D. Peters, took an interest in the project beyond the call of duty. Anne Cowlin helped with typing the initial drafts.

The Otis Elevator Company, part of United Technologies Corporation, sponsored a trip to New York and Chicago which helped with research on the history of the skyscraper and current trends, as well supplying original illustrations. My thanks to Dr Alaric Pugh of Peter Sawell & Partners for all the arrangements.

Lucy, my wife, and daughter Polly, put up with the seemingly endless midnight patter of my typewriter, and with many trips away in the course of the preparation of the book – in Polly's case from the day she entered the world. My special thanks to them for their understanding and endurance.

Charles Knevitt
Teddington, Middlesex
July 1985

COLOUR
ILLUSTRATIONS

INTRODUCTION

ARCHITECTURE AT THE THRESHOLD

Well-building hath three conditions: Commodity, Firmness, and Delight.
SIR HENRY WOTTON
Elements of Architecture (1624)
Adapted from Vitruvius, Book I, Chapter 3

If architecture is to be of service, it must respond to more than need. The architect must also serve desire; the desire of the building to be what it wants to be and the desire of the human being for self-expression. In serving desire, architecture contributes to the spiritual enrichment of the world.
JOHN LOBELL
Between Silence and Light: Spirit in the Architecture of Louis I. Kahn (1979)

All changed, changed utterly: A terrible beauty is born.
YEATS

The central tower of the Forth railway bridge, completed in 1890: a symbol of the new technology which was to be the most potent tool of modern architects.

Everyone has opinions about modern architecture, yet few people in Britain would be able to name more than one or two of the country's leading architects. People may sense that architects are not solely to blame for the sorry state of the environment, but at the same time suspect that they are collectively the professional group most responsible. Architects, after all, do design buildings – all too often buildings which people do not like, discussed in a language which they do not understand. There is a deep gulf between consumer and provider, one that an advanced society such as ours is increasingly finding intolerable.

There is widespread dissatisfaction that towns and cities have been transformed beyond recognition by 'experts', in the name of progress. All too frequently the Brave New Worlds created on countless drawing boards have become a living nightmare for those who have to live in or near them. The net result of the post-war building boom, of the Welfare State, and of property speculation has been the bleakness we see in most of our urban areas: unavoidable evidence of a lack of flair and imagination unequalled in the history of architecture. Almost too late, the cry 'Enough!' has gone up, to be followed inevitably by an understandable loss of confidence in the future and an unhealthy desire to hang on to the apron strings of the past.

More has been built in the last hundred years than in the whole of previous recorded history. The only certainty, American architect Philip Johnson has observed, is that building is about change. We live in a period of unprecedented change. Architecture is an unavoidable art, because we all need somewhere to live, work and play, but it is a *social* art, not an *abstract* one. Buildings give tangible expression to the values, priorities and aspirations of our society. But our relationship to them has also changed because of the pace of new development, the involvement of specialists in an increasingly complicated process of decision-making and control, and the fact that the scale of what has been built has dwarfed the individual. 'We shape our buildings,' Churchill said, 'but afterwards our buildings shape us.'

Since classical times, man has consciously built in relation to human proportions. The Doric, Ionic and Corinthian orders of the Greeks were explained in terms of human forms, with dimensions co-ordinated to represent, for example, how a man's foot was one-sixth of his height, and a woman's one-eighth. The Renaissance architect Alberti (1402–72) borrowed from that tradition as a result of reading the work of the Roman architect and theorist, Vitruvius, and illustrated the human figure at the centre of a circle and square, with hands and feet extended to symbolise man in harmony with the universe and at the centre of the world, an image later used by Leonardo. Palladio went a stage further and emphasised that the relationship of the parts of a building to each other, and of the parts to the whole, was at the root of beauty. His theories were to have an enormous impact on British architecture through Inigo Jones and Wren, and on those Georgian buildings which represent probably the best-loved period of our domestic architecture.

Owing to such things as town planning hurdles it is perhaps not surprising that buildings tend to be designed not to give delight, but to achieve minimum displeasure. There may be an understandable fear of architects and the jargon they use to convince you of your unutterable ignorance is decidedly off-putting for a potential patron. What we need now, therefore, are many more people refusing to be put off and demanding a creative dialogue between the architect and patron where both truly care about the quality of the end product. Only then will we see a reawakening of the patron's sense of responsibility, in that the results of his work will have an impact on the many people who use, live alongside or simply pass the building. Good architecture is not a luxury, nor need it be more expensive. Developers are coming to realise that good design produces a sound investment, while good patrons produce even better architects.
HRH THE PRINCE OF WALES
addressing the
Institute of Directors' annual convention (1985)

Left: Sir Joseph Paxton who designed the Crystal Palace for the Great Exhibition of 1851.

Opposite: Man in harmony with the universe and at the centre of the world. Leonardo's drawing takes up a theme explored by classical architects, including Vitruvius, and the Renaissance architect Alberti.

Above: The Crystal Palace, 1,800 ft long and covering 19 acres, was prefabricated and erected in just six months.

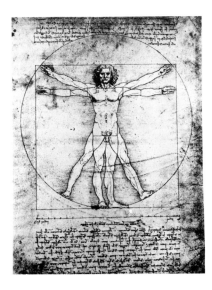

The Industrial Revolution ushered in man's ability to manufacture all his material needs and to control his environment. The achievement of such aims, however, cannot be made without cost; the cost, which we are heirs to, has been that twentieth-century man, far from exercising total mastery over industry and technology, has had to succumb to control by technology itself. Technology, insofar as it affected architecture, won its first victory in the middle of the nineteenth century, thanks to the inspired rationality of Sir Joseph Paxton. Arguably the most influential building of that century, his Crystal Palace for the Great Exhibition of 1851 was an inspired example of engineering rather than architecture.

Paxton was first and foremost a gardener, but at Chatsworth in Derbyshire he designed greenhouses, the largest being 300 ft long, in which he tried out a new method of glass and metal roofing. His move into architecture came almost by chance when he submitted a design, uninvited, for the Exhibition building. Not only was his the most 'rational' solution to covering the huge area of 19 acres in such a direct and obvious manner: he had also designed the 1,800-ft-long building in such a way as to allow prefabrication of all the elements, which could be made in factories and assembled on site in the space of just six months.

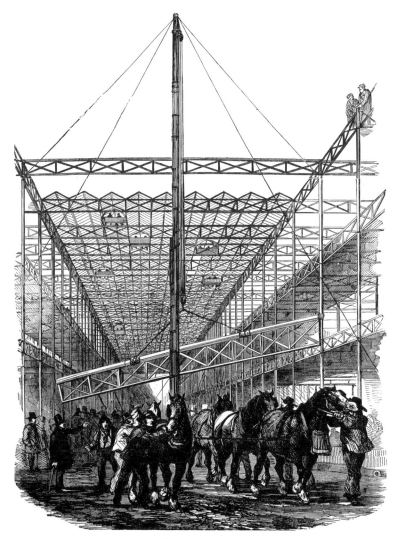

The fundamental failure of modern architecture was that in the shift from an agrarian society to an industrialised society, from handicrafts to the machine, from single production to mass production, in trying to produce in abundance for all the people, the people themselves got left out.
JOHN PORTMAN
(1984)

Paxton had unwittingly started the idea that technology could 'solve the problem' of quickly constructed and affordable buildings, an idea fundamental to the 'Modern Movement' of architecture, the key elements of which were the use of new materials and building techniques, forms stripped of ornament and decoration, and exploiting the new methods of construction to create a sense of space and light freed from the constraints of traditional materials. It also had social ideals: improving living and working conditions for everybody.

Architect Theo Crosby has described the Modern Movement as primarily 'an attempt to adjust architecture to new technologies', in which the structure of a building is allowed to express its own aesthetic, whether in iron, steel or concrete (i.e. construction technique and overall design should inter-relate).

At St Pancras station, the world's largest span was vaulted in 1868:

Xerox: A trademark for a photocopying device that can make rapid reproductions of human error, perfectly.
MERLE L. MEACHAM

Beauty in architecture has to be sought from within a world comprising 'a welter of commercial and municipal monstrosities. It is as though one had to tune a violin in the midst of a railway accident'.
GEOFFREY SCOTT
The Architecture of Humanism (1914)

243 ft of cast iron. In Paris, the Eiffel Tower of 1889 rose 985 ft (300m), also in cast iron. Skeleton construction of iron or steel gave birth to the skyscraper; the services technology of lifts and air conditioning made it work. But architecture soon found itself being dictated to by technology, by what machines could do well. Mass production of a limited range of standard elements took over and subsumed the individual and the unique.

St Pancras station: Sir George Gilbert Scott's hotel and offices, completed in 1876, are a riot of Gothic Revival architecture, in complete contrast to the train-shed roofs (*below*), which span 243 ft in cast iron. This was the largest span in the world when finished in 1868.

St Pancras Station

There is no relief or quiet in any part of the work. The eye is constantly troubled and tormented, and the mechanical patterns follow one another with such rapidity and perseverance, that the mind becomes irritated where it ought to be gratified and goaded to criticism where it should be led calmly to approve. There is here a complete travesty of noble associations, and not the slightest care to save these from sordid contact. An elaboration that might be suitable for a chapter-house, or a Cathedral choir, is used as an 'advertising medium' for bagmen's bedrooms and the costly discomforts of a terminus hotel, and the architect is thus a mere expensive rival of the Company's head cook in catering for the low enjoyments of the great travelling crowd . . . Here the public taste has been exactly suited, and every kind of architectural decoration has been made throroughly common and unclean.

J. M. EMMETT
quoted in *Victorian Architecture*
by John Summerson

The subsequent history of architecture has much to do with the expression of the architect's individuality – with technology his principal tool – at the expense of the user's individuality. Today's architect designs in a language which the 'ordinary' man does not understand, and in which he has no part.

In the Lethaby lectures given by Crosby at the Royal College of Art in 1975, which he called 'The Pessimist Utopia', he listed the imperatives underlying the Modern Movement, and asked his audience to consider whether they thought them still relevant. These were:

Left: The architect as hero: Gary Cooper as Howard Roark in the film of Ayn Rand's novel *The Fountainhead*.

Right: The architect as failed hero: Paul Newman clinging on for dear life in a scene from *Towering Inferno*.

>We live in a mass society
>Economy of scale
>Bigger is better
>Man at the centre
>Form follows function
>History is bunk
>Art is not decoration; and
>　decoration is not art
>The city is evil
>Universal mobility
>Sincerity is more important
>　than mere beauty
>The expert knows best

As architecture proliferated, it lost its integrity. At one point some of it succumbed to perpetual progress, never to recover . . . [from] the progressive-aggressive profession whose unattractive products are uppermost in our mind, if only for their inherent uppishness.
BERNARD RUDOFSKY
The Prodigious Builders (1977)

Such phrases formed a kind of collective unconscious, argued Crosby, which virtually guaranteed further depredations: for example, the destruction of cities by new roads in order to allow universal mobility, or the huge scale of new developments because 'bigger must be better' – and cheaper. Yet our preoccupation with progress, material benefits, and personal comfort and convenience had clouded our perception of what was going wrong. The failure of modern architecture can be seen in terms of what a leading article in *The Times* called 'some kind of atrocity committed in the face of the people, a technology-infatuated aberration from the true and traditional principles of architecture'. It went on: 'It is the crowning and expensive irony that these products of the technical approach to social action should have proved to an alarming extent themselves technically defective.'

Spectacular technological failures have been more than equalled by the social failure of various building types such as tower blocks for families, and the visual offensiveness and sensory deprivation of much of what has been built. The words of Seneca in the first century AD are grimly relevant today: 'That was a happy age, before the days of architects, before the days of builders.' Undoubtedly the biggest failure of the Modern Movement has been in the very area which was dearest to the hearts of politicians, planners and architects, in fulfilling one of the social goals of the Modern Movement: mass housing. It began in earnest after the First World War, when there was a need to build faster than traditional materials and skills would permit. In 1921, the young Le Corbusier pleaded for mechanisation in construction and produced some convincing words and images which were to have their greatest impact thirty years later in the reconstruction of Europe after the Second World War.

In 1919, Walter Gropius had founded the Bauhaus (literally 'building-house' or 'School of Building'), with the aim of integrating 'arts' and 'crafts'. It succeeded a school founded thirteen years earlier in Weimar based on the teaching of Ruskin and Morris of the English Arts and Crafts Movement. The Bauhaus manifesto began, 'The ultimate aim of all creative activity is the building.'

However, the original idea of integrating the skills of artist, craftsman and architect was ousted by a concern for industrial design and mass production.

Despite this change of emphasis, Gropius insisted on rigorous standards of design and quality control of all factory-produced components. Subsequent decades, however, witnessed an unfortunate progressive decline in manufacturing and building standards.

Mass production suddenly made possible buildings of an unprecedented scale, whether the Great Exhibition building, or the earliest skyscrapers of Chicago and New York. Complete buildings could be fitted out ready to be 'plugged in' to on-site services, power and water supplies and drainage. But what started as an idealistic dream of making good building available to all ended up as a monster beyond its creators' control.

That which distils, preserves and then enlarges the experience of a people is literature: and though I do not seek to absolve architects of their misdemeanours, I submit this thesis that with kitchen sink literature, it was natural that kitchen sink architecture would follow. If you seek their monument just look around you.
H. D. F. KITTO
The Greeks

The twin towers of Marina City, Chicago, have been described as 'corn on the cobs'. The repetitive use of a standard flat design and materials gives it the appearance of a product of modern technology.

The self-sufficiency of the specialist's world is a prisoner's illusion. It is time to open the gates.
LEWIS MUMFORD

All professions are conspiracies against the laity.
GEORGE BERNARD SHAW
The Doctor's Dilemma

For far too long, it seems to me, some planners and architects have consistently ignored the feelings and wishes of the mass of ordinary people in this country ... To be concerned about the way people live; about the environment they inhabit and the kind of community that is created by that environment should surely be one of the prime requirements of a really good architect.
HRH THE PRINCE OF WALES
addressing architects
at Hampton Court Palace (1984)

Mac's cartoon in the *Daily Mail* following comments by The Prince of Wales on modern architecture at Hampton Court Palace in 1984: 'For heaven's sake, Charles! He's only a child!'

The reaction against modern architecture on purely aesthetic grounds was stronger in Britain than in virtually any other country. 'England dislikes and distrusts revolution,' wrote Nikolaus Pevsner; although Modern Movement architecture was made possible by the Industrial Revolution, it was not evident on a large scale in Britain until shortly after the Second World War. It still remains alien to many people who have to live with its derivatives.

Continental architects welcomed industrialisation of the building industry as a means of realising the ancient dream of the Cathederal builders – to try to create interior spaces with light. Yet in Britain Ruskin and Morris had been turning to medievalism. By the end of the First World War, although it could not reconcile itself to the fact, Britain had started to lose its Empire. A harping-back to a traditionally glorious past offered a safer and more secure alternative than seeking a bright new future. Yet the architecture of the Industrial Revolution, which we now admire, was essentially utilitarian: the spinning mill, the dock warehouse, the iron bridge and, despite its elegance, the Crystal Palace itself. Pevsner, in *The Englishness of English Art,* remarked that no other country made so great a distinction between the utilitarian and the ornamental.

Architecture is not a fine art. It has a direct bearing on people's lives, and should therefore be influenced by them. 'Professionalism' sometimes intervenes; George Bernard Shaw went so far as to assert 'all professions are conspiracies against the laity'. Professionalism is essentially a nineteenth-century concept, one of 'the learned man' or 'expert'. The Royal Institute of British Architects, for example, was founded in 1834.

To many, the attitude of the professional architect was best summed

up by Owen Luder when President of the RIBA, in his inauspicious remarks about the entries for the extension to the National Gallery in Trafalgar Square in 1982. He suggested that the competition judges should choose the entry by Richard Rogers, because in Luder's view, Rogers is a man who has said, 'That is what I think the answer is, and sod you.' In so doing, he merely confirmed the widely held view of architects as arrogant and indifferent to the views of the man in the street.

While the last hundred and fifty years have seen great progress in almost every field of technology – electricity, telecommunications, mechanised flight, the motor car, radio and television, the microchip and putting a man on the moon – the nineteenth-century concept of the professional architect has hardly changed at all. What has changed is the nature of the clients, who are now corporations – public and private – rather than individuals.

In *The Image of the Architect,* Andrew Saint explains how the ideology and training of the architect have emphasised individualism and artistic ability to the detriment of organisational and co-operative talents, the comprehension of building techniques, and social responsibility. The net result has been that architects are regarded as impractical idealists. Society will not tolerate that intellectual elitism any longer. Architects will have to start sharing their knowledge and expertise, becoming more accountable to the public and more responsive to their needs.

Architects suffer from 'form fixation': Charles Jencks, the architectural historian, for example, remarked (after Mao Tse-tung), 'Architectural power grows out of the barrel of a 4B pencil,' epitomising the view that form is more influential than fitness for purpose. Forms are copied whether appropriate or not for a particular project, and reproduced almost unthinkingly: an example is the construction of skyscrapers in developing countries where there are no obvious pressures to build high.

'Our own system of financial, planning, and building controls is a remarkable and complex instrument,' wrote Theo Crosby, 'though it produces some terrible melodies. It needs tuning, and above all it needs to be made responsive.' He is really calling for an architecture of democracy, a vision shared by other architects and writers, such as Edward Cullinan, Ralph Erskine, and Jane Jacobs, as we shall see in later chapters. There is no reason why it has to remain elusive. Positive steps are being taken in the field of 'community architecture', in self-help and self-build schemes. The method of commissioning buildings has started to revert to the 'old pattern': client and architect collaborate to fulfil the client's needs. In their relationship with architecture, people are simultaneously 'actor and spectator', said Crosby. Perhaps we should ask ourselves, when each new plan is put forward, *who* will benefit, and whether it will improve the environment. Every project would then be measured on a scale of social desirability. It would then be once again legitimate for everyone to take part in design and planning

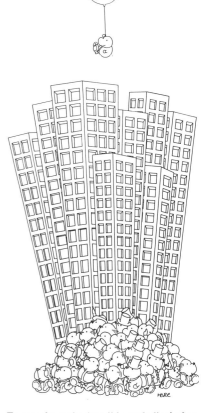

Escape from the 'terrible melodies' of an environment created by mass production techniques and a system of financial, planning and building controls: 'Follow me' by the Maltese cartoonist, Marc England.

Planners and architects are hooked on objects, and long for stable societies, for correct and accepted precedent within which a professional performance can be judged and applauded.
THEO CROSBY
How to Play the Environment Game (1973)

It has been said that 'the course of every intellectual, if he pursues his journey unflinchingly enough, ends in the obvious, from which the non-intellectuals have never stirred'.
LIONEL BRETT, VISCOUNT ESHER
Our Selves Unknown (1985)

If architects have a professional future at all it is (in the phrase of Geoffrey Vickers) as 'skilled understanders enabling people to work out their problems'.
COLIN WARD
addressing architectural students
in Sheffield (1976)

decisions without fear of trespassing on the professional's hallowed ground.

There are no absolutes in architecture, only degrees of understanding. Many see the current period of confusion and loss of nerve as a dead end, but architecture is an evolutionary process, and if the lessons of past mistakes can be learnt, then we should really see our present position as the threshold of a new and exciting era signified by social responsibility, opportunities for personal initiative, and self-help schemes of various kinds.

The complexities of contemporary life make the specialist's role an essential one, but he must ensure that his skills are used to aid the individual. The environmental and building professions should be responsive to people's needs and aspirations, 'enabling' them to help themselves rather than 'providing' what the experts think are the right solutions.

CHAPTER ONE

'A NICE PLACE TO BE'

What is the city but the people?
SHAKESPEARE
(Sicinius to the citizens of Rome, *Coriolanus,* Act III)

The human animal requires a spatial territory in which to live that possesses unique features, surprises, visual oddities, landmarks and architectural idiosyncracies. Without them it can have little meaning. A neatly symmetrical, geometric pattern may be useful for holding up a roof, or for facilitating the prefabrication of mass-produced housing units, but when such patterning is applied at the landscape level, it is going against the nature of the human animal. Why else do children prefer to play on rubbish dumps or in derelict buildings, rather than on their immaculate, sterile, geometrically arranged playgrounds?
DESMOND MORRIS
The Human Zoo
(1969)

I was all in a flutter at having at last got to the place which I was so madly fond of.
JAMES BOSWELL
London Journal (19 November 1762)

The Eiffel Tower, like the Pompidou Centre, is all bones and no skin. It took almost a century for Parisians and tourists to accept it as epitomising the city.

Most people live in towns and cities, so any consideration of architecture, people and buildings can most logically begin there.

A city is defined and given identity by places – buildings and the spaces around and in between them. The most important ones to a visitor or citizen are the gathering points, whether or not the individual buildings around them have any intrinsic design quality. A city needs a focus, a stage or public arena. This is the setting for the 'people' who are the 'city'.

Cathedral squares of medieval towns were often the scene of civic as well as religious celebrations, and Greek and Roman cities provided models for ambitious town planning schemes like Pope Sixtus V's baroque Rome, Baron Haussmann's Paris, or the Commissioner's Plan for imposing a grid on Manhattan Island. All of these have left a permanent imprint on those cities.

Consider these well-known public spaces: St Mark's Square in Venice, the Ponte Vecchio and the Piazza Della Signoria in Florence; Rockefeller Plaza in New York; and the square in front of the Pompidou Centre in Paris. London has Covent Garden Market and Leicester Square, but the city's two best known public spaces, Piccadilly Circus and Trafalgar Square, have long since been sacrificed to the motorcar. These public spaces have a unique identity, scale and intimacy which is attractive. They draw together many different types of people, doing many different things: going to and from work, shopping, eating or drinking out, sightseeing or simply observing and wanting to be observed. Humans are essentially gregarious.

How successful are modern architects in providing attractive public spaces? A useful comparison can be made between the South Bank in London and the area around the Pompidou Centre in Paris. Traditionally, the South Bank had been London's playground, with entertainment of all kinds from dancing bears to Shakespeare's Globe Theatre. In the aftermath of the Second World War, Herbert Morrison, Deputy

St Mark's Square, Venice, and the spaces around it, is one of the world's great 'people places' (to quote Richard Rogers's phrase) – a nice place to be.

Venice is like eating an entire box of chocolate liqueurs in one go.
TRUMAN CAPOTE
(26 November 1961)

I am not talking about blueprints or development plans, and all that committee fodder that gathers dust in municipal archives, but more about imagery. Throughout history, from the vision of battlemented white towers on a distant hill as in Renaissance painting, to the glitter and raucous vulgarity of New York's Broadway in the 1930s – 'the city' has been an idea to quicken the pulse and lift the heart; it is a quality of excitement which London on a warm spring evening still abundantly has. . . . To retain, or regain their magnetism, cities are going to have to adapt to new economic facts of life in ways we can only dimly perceive at present.
ANNE SOFER
GLC councillor
The Times (14 May 1984)

Prime Minister, suggested celebrating Britain's modern achievements in arts and sciences by building a temporary exhibition for the 1951 Festival of Britain. It was also to be a celebration of the centenary of the Great Exhibition. Although people were initially sceptical about 'Morrison's folly', it proved to be a great success, attracting eight and a half million visitors.

Sir Hugh Casson, its Architectural Director, recalled that it marked an era of optimism and reaction against the war-time drabness of khaki and camouflage. So the architecture of the Dome of Discovery, the Skylon, the pavilions and cafés, reflected the atmosphere of the period through its use of technology, colour and sense of fun. It was a dynamic place for as long as it lasted, occupying 27 acres between Waterloo Bridge and County Hall, with only the Royal Festival Hall conceived as a permanent building.

But when the last buildings of the Festival had been swept away, the area was developed as a cultural centre, unintentionally elitist rather than popular. The Hayward Gallery and later the National Theatre were built in the hard and aggressive sculptural forms of British Brutalism. The South Bank became a cultural ghetto, a single-function place in use for only part of the day. It was somewhere to pass through as quickly as possible rather than somewhere to linger and enjoy. Opportunities were missed, especially in the Hayward, to turn riverside terraces into

A particularly exciting project would be to convert the South Bank culture estate by adding, say, 1,000 dwellings, a shopping complex and pubs onto the same land presently occupied by the National Theatre, Hayward buildings and Festival Hall. The terraces and riverside could be exploited as amenities and leisure resources would then be valued to a fuller extent 24 hours a day!
TERRY FARRELL
'Buildings as a Resource'
RIBA Journal (May 1976)

The Festival of Britain of 1951 on London's South Bank. It demonstrated that modern architecture could be fun, but it was swept away to be replaced by concrete temples to high culture.

open-air exhibition spaces, cafés and restaurants. The buildings were largely blind to the River Thames flowing by them, and the grey bunkers of concrete and high-level walkways, devoid of purpose and badly signposted, became forbidding and alienating.

The chief architectural inspiration for the pile of concrete blocks on the South Bank appears to have been a cross between Speer's Atlantic Wall and the Führerbunker.
CHRISTOPHER BOOKER
'Dreams that crack like concrete' (1976)

Cities, like cats, will reveal themselves at night.
RUPERT BROOKE
Letters from America

'Thamesday', an annual event on London's South Bank, is the only time (apart from evenings) when the place comes alive with people and activity.

Three million people a year visit the South Bank, but the area comes to life only in the evening and during the annual 'Thamesday' event. There have been recent attempts to introduce more of a busy, carnival atmosphere throughout the day, by extending the opening hours of the cafés at the National Film Theatre and the Royal Festival Hall. What the area needs, however, are activities and events which can ensure daily use by local people, commuters and visitors.

The National Theatre, designed by Sir Denys Lasdun in the hard and aggressive sculptural form of British Brutalism. Its foyers work extremely well and give an alluring glimpse to passers-by at night, but in daylight many find its concrete exterior uninviting – even forbidding.

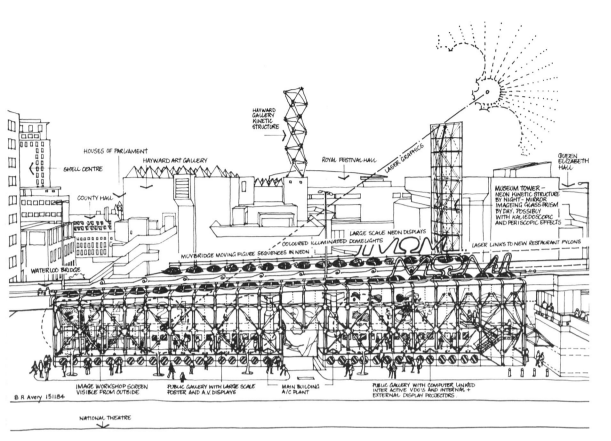

HAYWARD GALLERY KINETIC STRUCTURE

HOUSES OF PARLIAMENT

HAYWARD ART GALLERY

ROYAL FESTIVAL HALL

LASER GRAPHICS

SHELL CENTRE

QUEEN ELIZABETH HALL

COUNTY HALL

MUSEUM TOWER – NEON KINETIC STRUCTURE BY NIGHT – MIRROR IMAGEING GLASS PRISM BY DAY, POSSIBLY WITH KALIEDOSCOPIC AND PERISCOPIC EFFECTS

LARGE SCALE NEON DISPLAYS

COLOURED ILLUMINATED DOMELIGHTS

WATERLOO BRIDGE

MUYBRIDGE MOVING FIGURE SEQUENCES IN NEON

LASER LINKS TO NEW RESTAURANT PYLONS

B R Avery 151184

IMAGE WORKSHOP SCREEN VISIBLE FROM OUTSIDE

PUBLIC GALLERY WITH LARGE SCALE POSTER AND A.V. DISPLAYS

MAIN BUILDING A/C PLANT

PUBLIC GALLERY WITH COMPUTER LINKED INTER ACTIVE V.D.U'S AND INTERNAL + EXTERNAL DISPLAY PROJECTORS.

NATIONAL THEATRE

Architect Bryan Avery's design for the Museum of the Moving Image, intended for completion by late 1987.

The indescribable is enacted here.
The choir of angels
talking about heaven in
Faust by
J. W. VON GOETHE

When I was a child the streets of any city
were full of street vendors and street
entertainers of every kind, and of the
latter the Italian organ-grinder with his
monkey was one of the most endearing.
Today, officialdom seems to have
banished them all, and the only persons
who still earn their living on the streets
are prostitutes and dope peddlers.
W. H. AUDEN
A Certain World

The opening of the Museum of the Moving Image next to the National Film Theatre, scheduled for the autumn of 1987, should help. The museum, full of exhibits in which observers can take part, should itself draw more than one million extra visitors a year. The design by Bryan Avery is open-sided, glazed, and inviting – in stark contrast to its neighbours.

The Pompidou Centre at Beaubourg in Paris is an area of quite a different character to the South Bank: colourful, dynamic, accessible. Inside is a library containing half a million books and as many slides, films, television and video programmes and records. It's the home of both permanent and changing exhibitions, and of an experimental music workshop.

Renzo Piano and Richard Rogers designed this massive structure – each floor is the size of two football pitches – as a place to integrate art into everyday life. They acknowledged the influence on their design of architect Cedric Price's plans for a London 'Fun Palace' – a multi-activity, multi-media centre – which was never built. The Pompidou Centre is closer to ship and aircraft technology than conventional building. Contemporary technology has created, as it did in the Eiffel Tower a century earlier, a dramatic, controversial and exciting building. When it opened in 1977, the £100-million centre was expected to be

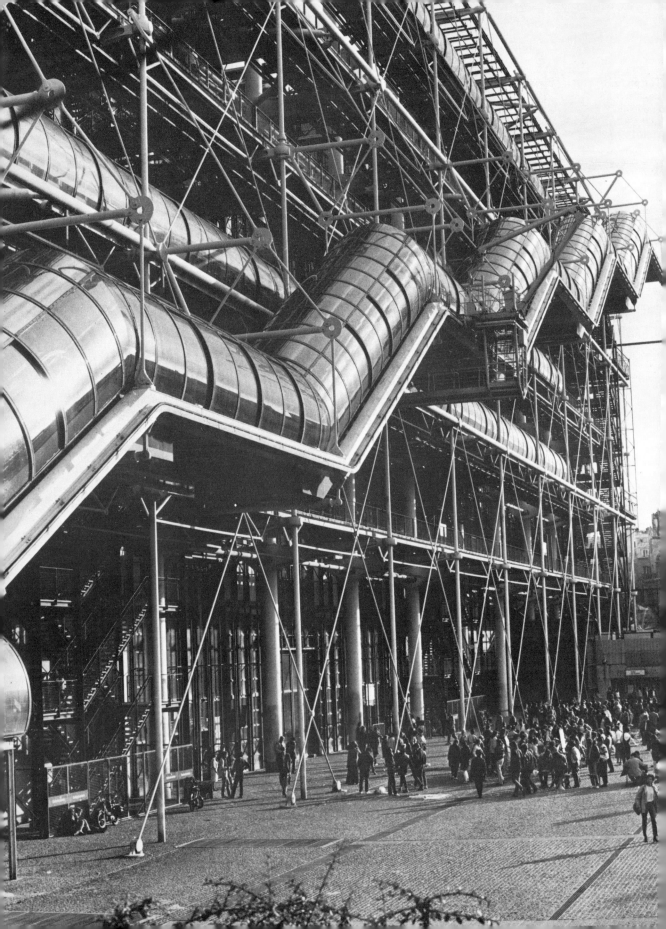

The multi-use Pompidou Centre at Beaubourg in Paris: colourful, dynamic and inviting. It is a modern counterpart to the Eiffel Tower in its exploitation of technology to produce architecture as an event. (See colour photograph, p. 34)

used by about two thousand people a day: it soon attracted twenty thousand, and two million visited it in the first two years, a figure which outstripped the Eiffel Tower and Louvre combined. Subsequent attendance figures have reached eight million per year.

The Pompidou Centre is architecture as an event. Rogers describes it as more of a market place than a building; a 'people place' as he puts it. Its exterior is painted in the colours of a French *Tricolore:* red for the lift housing, white for the ventilation ducts and blue for the other mechanical equipment.

It is impossible to be equivocal about the place; people either love it or hate it. (Spike Milligan, one of the latter category remarked, 'The only good thing about that building is that it's in Paris'.) Unlike the stark formality of the South Bank, to which people can be indifferent, the

To err is human, To loaf is Parisian.
VICTOR HUGO
Les Misérables (1862)

Cedric Price's design for a London 'Fun Palace', a multi-activity, multi-media centre which influenced the Piano and Rogers design of the Pompidou Centre. The second picture shows how it might appear to someone arriving by helicopter.

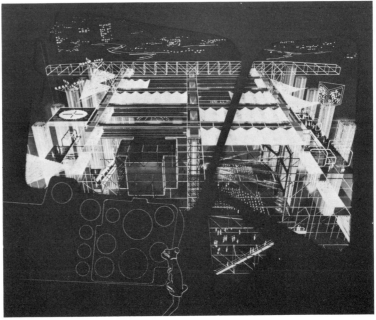

Architecture is in a sense a microcosm of the city.
DENYS LASDUN
Architecture in an Age of Scepticism (1984)

Art history

Information theory decodes a message as a field of elements into binary digits (BIT). We can thus quantify the aesthetic information (i.e. optical challenges) in an architectonic message. Perception is stimulated by gaining aesthetic information. The beholder has to reduce a vast number of optical challenges to the restricted capacity of our visual memory (160 BIT) before he can observe details. The drawing shows the progressive simplifications required to see an historic house. Read the other way it shows the increase in aesthetic information between levels of complexities. An 'interesting' environment is characterized by a high level of aesthetic information, using a large vocabulary of different elements. Modern buildings, lacking associative potentiality, offer particularly low quantities of information and lose our interest in the first simplification.

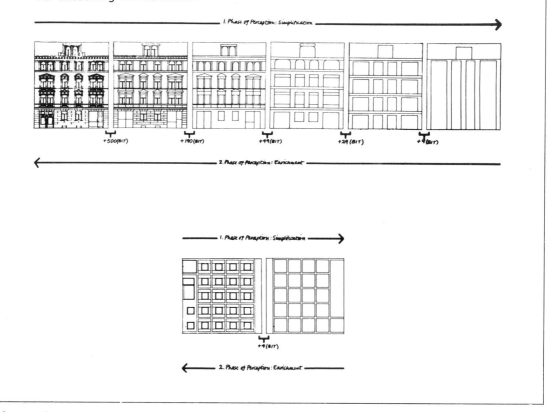

fairground atmosphere of the Pompidou Centre makes an impact. Whether or not one enjoys the Hi-Tech character of the Piano and Rogers Building, it is visually interesting and therefore memorable. (Theo Crosby explains the information-theory basis of this in the accompanying illustration.) People complain that modern buildings are

Theo Crosby's analysis of the visual language of 'old' and 'modern' architecture, as described in his exhibition and book, *How to Play the Environment Game* (1973).

The town is new every day.
ESTONIAN PROVERB

'The Queen and the Washerwomen of Brandon Hill' by Walter Ritchie, carved intaglio in Italian marble in the National Westminster Bank, Corn Street, Bristol. Ritchie continues the tradition of sculpture as an art form to enrich people's everyday lives.

'boxes', 'anonymous' or 'dull', because they are not sufficiently distinctive from one another. Visual intricacies are amongst the ways in which we distinguish buildings from one another. Since the advent of the Modern Movement, few buildings have been embellished in any way. Ornament was banned as a 'crime' by the precursors of the Movement and is only now, with pattern, colour and decoration, re-entering our lives. Crosby's own scheme for the interior of Uniliver House in London is one example of the new ornamentation. (See colour illustration, p. 34.) Another example is Walter Ritchie's delightful sculpture, which appears in squares, churches, schools and banks.

Apart from containing few appropriate or interesting modern buildings, many cities have a further problem. In affluent societies, we have allowed the motorcar to assume such importance in our lives that it both limits our enjoyment of towns and cities, and distorts their development. Los Angeles is the extreme example. It has no area which can be called 'downtown', the centre. It is planned for private transport rather than public use and enjoyment. Two-thirds of the land area is devoted to roads or parking.

Britain, being an older, smaller country, has not allowed the car to shape its cities and towns to the same extent, but the planners of no large urban area have entirely avoided making some concessions to road transport. People have had to fight back to reclaim the city as their own.

Pedestrianisation of shopping precincts is one approach; earlier successes include Norwich, Hereford, Leeds and the Church Street area of Liverpool.

In Chester, pedestrianisation went hand in hand with an ambitious conservation strategy and an active urban regeneration programme devised by the architect Donald Insall for a 1968 Government study.

No city should be too large for a man to walk out of in the morning.
CYRIL CONNOLLY
The Unquiet Grave

If you would be known, and not know, vegetate in a village; if you would know, and not be known, live in a city.
CHARLES CALEB COTTON
Lacon (1825)

Modern architecture is a flop . . . There is no question that our cities are uglier today than they were fifty years ago.
PHILIP JOHNSON (1968)

The use of collage, multiplicity of images, dispersal of forms to create village or mini-city massing, episodic diversions into detail en route, the love of repetition of an understood vocabulary, the instinct not too arrive but to enjoy much more of the journey (Chaucer-style) are all anecdotal or narrative in structure and attitude. The labyrinthine narrative is a particularly exciting format: great buildings like Street's City of London Law Courts and Waterhouse's Manchester Town Hall, as well as whole areas of cities such as London, Chester and Edinburgh elaborately avoid the formal urban patterns of Europe and America. Colin Rowe reflected this particularly British tendency when he refers to buildings generally as 'speech' and architecture specifically as 'literature'.
TERRY FARRELL
Terry Farrell
Architectural Monographs (1984)

The Bear and Billet Hotel in Chester, one of the 'core' buildings kept in Donald Insall's programme.

If ever we are to have a time of architecture again, it must be founded on a love for the city. No planting down of a few costly buildings, ruling some straight streets, provision of fountains or setting up of stone, or bronze dolls is enough without the enthusiasm for corporate life and common ceremonial. Every noble city has a crystallization of the contentment, pride and order of the community.
W. R. LETHABY
(1857–1931)

The Great Victorian Way, designed by Sir Joseph Paxton in 1854 as a continuous glass-covered arcade, 10 miles long, encircling London.

The identity of the Bridgegate area, a former Roman citadel, required keeping the scale intact and treating historical buildings as a resource for repair and re-use. It was the first major study of a city as a living organism which needed nurturing, taking into account the many conflicting pressures of building owners, shop keepers and developers. Through a combination of public initiative and private enterprise, it became a model for others to follow.

Not only roads and thoroughfares can be dedicated to people. Even in the most densely developed areas of cities, there may be open spaces. Manhattan has Paley Park and Greenacre Park, known as 'vest-pocket parks' because of their tiny size. Both are islands of tranquillity in a sea of frantic activity, Paley especially so because it has a waterfall to provide a constant mask to traffic noise, and moveable seats and tables, where office workers and visitors to the city can eat sandwiches or sit and rest. Trade-offs between city authorities and developers can produce even more substantial contributions of public space; at Battery Park City in New York, currently under construction, there is no less than 300,000 sq. ft.

Given the vagaries of weather in Europe and America, it is a logical move to enclose such spaces. Architects have attempted to control the climate by building arcades. The idea is not as recent as it might appear.

In 1854, Paxton proposed a Great Victorian Way to encircle London. This was to be a continuous glass-covered arcade, 10 miles long, skirting the city along a route similar to that now traced by the Circle Line of the underground, of which development began 30 years after the Great Victorian Way was proposed. Shops and houses would run down each side of a 72-ft wide street for pedestrians and carriages, the same width as the transept of Paxton's Great Exhibition Building. Paxton also prophesied the air-conditioned environments of later shops and offices. He promised that temperatures would be regulated to 'give the whole of London a new source of comfort and enjoyment'. It would 'prevent many infirm persons being obliged to go into foreign countries in the winter'.

Milan had already experimented with an enclosed arcade in the Galleria de Cristoforis of 1832, 'all glass and mirrors', including the roof. In the same city, there was later built the greatest arcade ever, designed by Giuseppe Mengoni. He won a competition for the Galleria Vittorio Emanuele II although he had never studied architecture. Nearly a hundred shops, restaurants, cafés and bars filled the two covered streets, which took the form of a Latin cross, one 1,643 ft long, the other 344 ft, beneath the roofs 88 ft high, which meet at a central cupola 160 ft high.

Opposite top: **Covent Garden, London. A successful example of a new use of existing buildings: the former fruit and vegetable market in Covent Garden, London, built in 1830, is now a leisure-shopping centre drawing hundreds of thousands of tourists and visitors every year.**

Opposite bottom: **Regency Hotel, Atlanta. The atrium of the Hyatt Regency Atlanta Hotel, in Atlanta, Georgia, became a prototype for hotel design and many office buildings. John Portman's design includes glass-encased lifts, sculpture, planting, sitting areas and restaurant within a space 120 ft square and 23 storeys high, overlooked by balconies.**

Memory of travel is the stuff of our fairest dreams. Splendid cities, plazas, monuments and landscapes that pass before our eyes, and we enjoy again the charming and impressive spectacles that we have formerly experienced.
CAMILLO SITTE
The Art of Building Cities
(1945)

Whatever space and time mean, place and occasion mean more. For space in the image of man is place, and time in the image of man is occasion . . . Provide that place, articulate the in between . . . make a welcome of each door and a countenance of each window . . . get closer to the shifting centre of human reality and build its counterform – for each man and all men . . .
ALDO VAN EYCK

The Galleria Vittorio Emanuele II in Milan. Nearly a hundred shops, restaurants, cafés and bars fill two covered streets in the world's largest arcade.

Opposite top left: An example of the revival of decoration: Theo Crosby's refurbishment of the interior of Unilever House in London.

Opposite bottom left: The Galleria, Houston. One of the first mixed-use leisure-shopping malls in America is the Galleria in Houston. An indoor ice-skating rink provides a focus for shoppers, office workers, hotel guests and those using the art galleries, cinemas and restaurants which form part of the development.

Opposite right, top and *bottom*: Pompidou Centre, Beaubourg, Paris. Open, accessible and inviting, colourful, dynamic and most importantly, multi-use. A symbol of popular culture, it attracts about 20,000 visitors every day – more than the Eiffel Tower and Louvre combined. The exterior is painted in the colours of the French *Tricolore*: red for the lift housing, white for the ventilation extracts, and blue for other mechanical equipment. A series of glass-encased escalators snakes its way past open viewing platforms.

Right: The interior of the Ford Foundation Building in New York, designed by Kevin Roche and John Dinkerloo and completed in 1967. The atrium, open to the public, is enclosed on two sides by offices, and on two sides by glass.

But the present disreputable state of civitas *in the United States is the product of an exaggeratedly Calvinist sense of sin. Finding the city irredeemable is only the other side of the coin to expecting it to be Paradise: utopias and dystopias go, of necessity, hand in hand. Disillusion is a vital part of the process of dreaming – and may, one suspects, prove almost as enjoyable.*
JONATHAN RABAN
Soft City (1974)

The Galleria is a public thoroughfare, forming an important link between the cathedral and La Scala Opera House. It is open twenty-four hours a day, so has become part of the public space of the city, unlike the English arcades such as those in Leeds and Cardiff which opened shortly after the Milan Galleria.

In the twentieth century, American architects have further developed the enclosed public space. The Ford Foundation Building in New York, designed by Kevin Roche and John Dinkerloo, was completed in 1967. It brings together conservatory, office block, and public

arena in one building. It inspired many imitators, and also demonstrated that philanthropy could pay dividends. Offices take up only two sides, an L-shape, of the cube of space, while the rest rises 130 ft as an atrium filled with a luxuriant park open to the public.

John Portman consciously designs 'people places', but there can be no doubt that he has created some of the most impressive spaces in American architecture, worthy of the eighteenth-century fantasies of Piranesi. To some, Portman buildings are the height of elegance; to others they are vulgar. In his home town of Atlanta, in San Francisco, and in the Renaissance Center, Detroit, the Hyatt Regency hotel chain succeeded in turning the architect's daring visions to commercial advantage by an improved room occupancy rate. This was enlightened self-interest on a grand scale. Glass-encased lifts, hung on the outside of

their shafts, provide kinetic sculpture as well as breathtaking views for those travelling in them. Developers of mixed-use buildings soon realised the advantage of providing grand public spaces. In Houston, Texas, a Galleria designed by Hellmuth, Obata and Kassabaum combined specialty retail shops, a major department store, an office tower and luxury hotel with a three-storey covered shopping mall as its focus. The public, as well as visiting shops, can enjoy art galleries and ice rink, cinemas and restaurants, all under one roof. A similar building, the Omni-International in Atlanta, incorporates an Olympic-sized rink enclosed by fourteen-storey office blocks and a glazed roof.

When the company IDS approached Philip Johnson and John Burgee to design a city-centre office block in Minneapolis, the architects suggested that a mixed-use and spacially extravagant atrium made sense. They persuaded their client to add shops, and scatter the various buildings around the perimeter of the site, thus freeing 20,000

John Portman's dramatic atrium at the Hyatt Regency Hotel, San Francisco, includes formal public spaces, planting, sculpture, water, an aviary, and glass-encased lifts, as well as restaurants, shops and bars.

The world is still deceived with ornament.
SHAKESPEARE
The Merchant of Venice
Act III, Scene ii.

The city should be an organisation of love . . . the best economy in cities is the care and culture of men.
LEWIS MUMFORD

We will neglect our cities at our peril, for in neglecting them we neglect the nation.
JOHN F. KENNEDY
message to US Congress
(30 January 1962)

The city is a fact in nature, like a cave, a run of mackerel or an ant-heap. But it is also a conscious work of art, and it holds within its communal framework many simpler and more personal forms of art. Mind takes form in the city; and in turn, urban forms condition mind. For space, no less than time, is artfully reorganised in cities: in boundary lines and silhouettes, in the fixing of horizontal planes and vertical peaks, in utilizing or denying the natural site, the city records the attitude of a culture and an epoch to the fundamental facts of its existence. The dome and the spire, the open avenue and the closed court, tell the story, not merely of different physical accommodations, but of essentially different conceptions of man's destiny. The city is both a physical utility for collective living and a symbol of those collective purposes and unanimities that arise under such favouring circumstance. With language itself, it remains man's greatest work of art.
LEWIS MUMFORD
The Culture of Cities (1938)

Ninety-nine per cent of modern architecture [is] boring, banal, and barren, and usually disruptive and unharmonius when placed in older cities.
JAMES STIRLING
speaking at Yale University (1974)

The six-storey atrium at the Trump Tower in New York is filled with mirrored images of balconies, escalators and a giant waterfall sculpture, attracting custom to the shops and restaurants in it. (See also colour photograph p. 67.)

sq. ft at its centre for a covered court, acting as a route between activities around it and linking up with the surrounding streets and high-level pedestrian walkways.

So the Crystal Court was born, a 120-ft high area bounded by walls which glitter with mirrored saw-tooth zig-zags, reflecting one another, beneath a jumbled pyramid of cubic glass and plastic. In a city of extremes of temperature from season to season, the Crystal Court provides not only protection from the weather, but also a public space of some elegance and sophistication.

The climatically controlled atrium has rapidly become one of the most important features of late-twentieth-century architecture; the concept is continually being refined to provide indoor city spaces which are attractive in their own right. Visitors to the Trump Tower in New York are entertained by a pianist as they enter a six-storey atrium which has a waterfall cascading down the full height of a wall sculpture. Such attractions draw crowds to the centres, and so to surrounding shops, thus justifying the atria in strictly commercial terms.

Next to the Trump Tower, and linked to it, is the conservatory of the IBM Building, filled with bamboo plants, and tables and chairs – a trade-off for being allowed to build higher. Atria are natural meeting places, reintroducing the market-place/forum concept of the earliest, naturally evolved, cities.

In Chicago, at Water Tower Place, architect John Schlossman has created what he calls a 'third generation' shopping centre. It contains a series of inviting spaces leading up to the main concourse. Escalators lead through the plants and waterfalls to cantilevered balconies of shops, surrounding three hexagonal glass-encased lifts which provide a novel experience for shoppers.

Public atria are also being built into otherwise private buildings. Helmut Jahn's State of Illinois Centre in Chicago, for example, has one reminiscent of a NASA launching pad.

These public spaces are significant in view of the widespread concern recently felt about the future of the inner city. Atria, and in general buildings which make people feel welcome, can help stem the flight to the suburbs, encouraging people to enjoy social and business activities in urban surroundings once again.

Future possibilities have been suggested by Buckminster Fuller's geodesic domes, like that created for the American Pavilion at the Montreal Expo, or the much larger version intended to enclose several square miles of Manhattan (see p. 150).

In 1978, Norman Foster, who shares many of the late Fuller's concerns abut maximising the performance of materials and pushing technology to its limits, produced designs for the Hammersmith Centre in London. Here the atrium concept is exploded into a four-acre park surrounded by four walls of offices containing 600,000 sq. ft of space, and roofed over with a lightweight translucent membrane. In a way, it is

One cannot zone a steel rolling mill in the middle of a domestic housing area, but it is wrong to be too clinical in separating the various activities of a community. It tends to create an evening and weekend man, a work man, a shopping man and a recreational man; whereas at one time a community of whole men provided the necessary contact for complete social indentity.
Evidence given by
THE HIGH WYCOMBE SOCIETY
Buckinghamshire
to the UN Conference
on the Human Environment (June 1972)

Opposite: **Buckminster Fuller's geodesic dome for the American Pavilion at Expo 67, Montreal (which later burnt down). It gave an impression of what great urban spaces of the future could be like, if that architectural course is chosen.**

Below: **Norman Foster's design for the Hammersmith Centre, London, which would have a lightweight transparent roof covering a four-acre park between office blocks.**

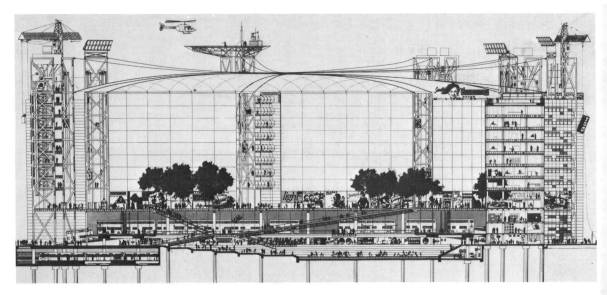

The interior of the Willis Faber Dumas headquarters building in Ipswich, by Norman Foster, a working environment designed to encourage social interaction.

Less is more.
MIES VAN DER ROHE
(*c.*1923)

Less is a bore.
ROBERT VENTURI
Complexity and Contradiction in Architecture (1966)

An imaginary city, Le Corbusier's Ville Radieuse, and a real one, Los Angeles, were built as shrines to the vision of the citizen as motorist. His changed scale of speed and distance gave rise to a city plan in which individuals were perceived as voyagers: the neighbourhood and the street were replaced by the super-highway, and the old supportive systems in which one knew who one was by the reflections given back by familiar faces from next door or the corner shop gave way to the bold, curt announcement of identity made by the motor car.
JONATHAN RABAN
Soft City (1974)

the same architect's Willis Faber and Dumas head office at Ipswich, but writ large. The Ipswich project emphasised the importance of making everday working environments 'nice places to be'. In his Hongkong and Shanghai bank (see pp. 79 and 199), he generates a feeling of participation and involvement in everything which is going on around the perimeter offices by the movement of people through the central 11-storey atrium on escalators placed diagonally across the space, and by 'glass lanterns' of lifts. A similar idea can be found in his former partner Richard Rogers's £157-million Lloyd's headquarters in the City of London.

If these are the best examples of places created by modern architects which the public view and enjoy, then what has happened to the visions of the Italian futurists – epitomised in Fritz Lang's film set for *Metropolis,* and Le Corbusier's town planning studies for skyscrapers set in parks, linked by motorways? These have proved to be self-fulfilling prophesies, but they also proved to be the antithesis of the city relevant to the citizens' needs.

One of the most significant aspects of these future visions was the idea of zoning. But the most successful cities contain diversity, disparate and haphazard activities occuring side by side. As Swedish architect Gunnar Apslund remarked, 'Urban intensity is like a fire which dies down if the logs are separated.'

If we look at what are probably the most successful examples of city planning – also 'nice places to be' – one is forced to acknowledge the

The planner is my shepherd. He maketh me to walk; through dark tunnels and underpasses he forceth me to go. He maketh concrete canyons tower above me. By the rivers of traffic he maketh me walk. He knocketh down all that is good, he maketh straight the curves. He maketh of the city a wasteland and a car park.
MIKE HARDING
'A Short Guide to Modern Architecture,' in *When the Martians Land in Huddersfield* (1984)

Human ants populate Le Corbusier's *Ville Radieuse* of 1930. The citizen is dominated by tall buildings, an airport and urban motorway. Not nowadays considered a very nice place to be.

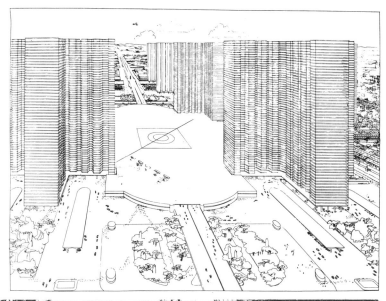

When you get there, there isn't any there there.
GERTRUDE STEIN
on Oakland

Sleeping Beauty Castle at Disneyland, along with Main Street, USA and other landmarks, is a self-conscious — and highly lucrative — re-creation of traditional friendly urban spaces.

attractiveness of such totally artificial places as Portmeirion or Disneyland.

The architect Clough Williams-Ellis created Portmeirion on the coast of North Wales as his private place. It was modelled on an Italian hill town, the squares, towers and terraces largely rebuilt from buildings demolished elsewhere. It became familiar to millions of television viewers as the setting of *The Prisoner* series.

Disneyland in California, and later Walt Disney World in Florida, are the most obvious attempts to recreate 'nice places to be' from scratch, and it is significant that they include familiar 'landmark' buildings,

Architecture is a social art and only makes sense as the promoter and extender of human relations.
DENYS LASDUN
quoted in
Contemporary Architects (1980)

It is in the city, the city as theater, that man's purposive activities are formulated and worked out, through conflicting and cooperating personalities, events, groups, into more significant culminations.
LEWIS MUMFORD
The Culture of Cities (1938)

Cities are sensitive, complex organisms which can be seriously harmed by ignorant interference and wholesale renewal. To plan properly for the future we must have a deep understanding of how things came to be as they are and the precise nature of the existing fabric.
ILLTYD HARRINGTON
Chairman of the Greater London Council:
Foreword to
London Surveyed 1894–1984 (1984)

Architecture is only part of the problem of cities. Conceivably we could have a great city of mediocre buildings. It might be a happy place in which to live. And you might have a beautiful city that is not a happy city.
ALLAN TEMKO
The City

Portmeirion, North Wales, created by the architect Clough Williams-Ellis from 1926 onwards. An 'Italian hill village' set against the backdrop of the peak of Snowdon, it was here that Nöel Coward wrote *Blithe Spirit*, and *The Prisoner* cult television series was filmed.

*The very turmoil of the streets has
something repulsive, something against
which human nature rebels. The
hundreds of thousands of all classes and
ranks crowding past each other, are they
not all human beings with the same
qualities and powers, and with the same
interest in being happy? . . . And still
they crowd by one another, and their only
agreement is the tacit one, that each keep
to his own side of the pavement, so as not
to delay the opposing streams of the
crowd, while it occurs to no man to
honour another with so much as a
glance.*
FRIEDRICH ENGELS
*The Condition of the Working Class in
England in 1844*

*The materials of city planning are sky,
space, trees, steel and cement in that
order and in that hierarchy.*
LE CORBUSIER
quoted in *The Times* (1965)

*The improvement in city conditions by the
general adoption of the motor-car can
hardly be over-estimated. Streets clean,
dustless and odorless, with light rubber-
tired vehicles moving swiftly and
noiselessly over their smooth expanse,
would eliminate a greater part of the
nervousness, distraction and strain of
modern metropolitan life.*
Scientific American
(1899)

*I am convinced that, after the
fundamental question of preserving
peace, it is the form and organisation or
urban areas that is now looming up as
the greatest social challenge for the world
for the rest of this century.*
COLIN BUCHANAN
Professor of Transport
Imperial College, London

squares, and 'Main Street USA'. Port Grimaud, the tourist village in the south of France, is equally an attempt at providing an artificial planned environment which reflects the qualities of traditional places in scale, materials, texture and informality. Many of these qualities, artificially created in those places, are natural ingredients of successful conversions of existing buildings for new uses, such as 'leisure shopping' (shopping for other than essentials). Fantasy worlds inter-relate with reality to an extent that we sometimes choose not to acknowledge: it's indicative that Harrods' slogan is 'Enter a Different World'.

It makes sense to keep and re-use places which people naturally feel comfortable in. Thus, Covent Garden Market in London, Ghirardelli Square and the Cannery in San Francisco, and Faneuil Market in Boston are discussed in the chapter on conservation. Places can also be created by happy accident, and the planners then have the sense to keep them. Rockefeller Plaza in New York is one such example. A sunken area meant originally as the entrance to the subway has become an ice-skating rink in winter and an outdoor café in summer. (See p. 165.)

It would seem that architects and planners are at last realising that the future of cities depends on the public being able to enjoy them – the city must belong to the people or it no longer functions as a city.

Woolworth Building. New York.

'The Cathedral of Commerce!' was how the Woolworth Building was described at its opening in 1913. President Woodrow Wilson switched on the 80,000 lights by pressing a button in the White House in Washington.

CHAPTER TWO

CATHEDRALS OF COMMERCE

America needs tall buildings.
It needs skyscrapers.
American Architect Magazine
(1883)

What need has thou of a monument?
Thou hast raised to thyself the most
glorious one! And though the ants that
scrabble around it trouble not about thy
name, thou hast a fate like to the master-
builder's who piled the mountainpeaks up
into the clouds!
To few was it granted to conceive in their
souls Babel-thoughts, complete, gigantic,
wholly lovely down to the finest part, like
the trees of God; to fewer still, to light
upon thousands of willing hands, to dig
out stony foundations, to conjure
towering structures thereupon, and then
in dying to say to their sons: I am with
you always in the works of my spirit –
carry on that which I have begun to its
consummation, high in the clouds!
J. W. VON GOETHE

Von Deutscher Baukunst (1772)
Goethe was writing about the
unfinished Gothic splendour of
Strasbourg Cathedral.

The most spectacular change in architecture has been brought about by the arrival of skyscrapers: to most people, they epitomise modern architecture. The word 'skyscraper' was first used to describe the tallest sail on a clipper ship, a high-flying bird, or a hit or tossed baseball. The correspondent of the *American Architect* was probably the first to use it to describe tall buildings. 'Cloudscraper', a term coined by a young Minneapolis architect L. S. Buffington, never really caught on.

The skyscraper is America's gift to architecture. The Home Insurance Building in Chicago was completed in the autumn of 1885, designed by William le Baron Jenney. It can probably claim to be the first true skyscraper, iron-framed and intended primarily for commercial use. Only a hundred years later, high-rise buildings have become universal in the developed world.

Significant developments in technology towards the end of the nineteenth century made it feasible to build high in response to the growing demand for office space. As a result, the skyscraper came to express the corporate identity of burgeoning enterprises, and the egos of those who controlled them. The commercial ambitions of New York and Chicago have shaped their physical identities. They are a source of pride for their citizens, and a great rivalry still continues. Skyscrapers have been condemned as inhuman in scale, but that is not an inherent fault. They are all too often built as evidence of 'progress', rather than because they are a necessary solution to the problem of providing working and living space in confined areas.

Only in comparatively recent times have towers been associated with land speculation and prestige. Historically, they signify a religious expression and civic celebration. The round towers of Ireland, dating from about AD 400, and of which some sixty-five still survive, were erected for security. The twelfth-century tower at Ardmore, County Waterford, rises 97 ft; its entrance is 15 ft up its side so as to deter intruders.

'Tower of Babel' (detail) as depicted by Pieter Bruegel I (c.1525–69). The world's first skyscraper?

The twelfth-century Ardmore Tower, County Waterford, rises 97 ft. Its entrance is 15 ft above the ground to deter intruders.

In Italy, the towers of the Tuscan town of San Gimignano indicated wealth and identity, and were sometimes used as family-sized fortifications. Bologna once boasted two hundred towers. The 323-ft Torve Asinelli, built in 1109, still stands guard.

In the western Caucasus (Russia), there are defence towers, sometimes built singly, at other times in forests of fifty or sixty.

In most cases the material used for these towers is stone, but clay models discovered by archaeologists suggest that the ancient Assyrians may have lived in ten-storey structures built with load-bearing skeletons of wood. These designs even have set-backs, a feature which re-emerged in the early-twentieth-century zoning regulations of New York and Chicago, then intended to ensure light between canyons created by office blocks.

The idea of using prefabricated sections for rapid assembly is not new either. A twenty-storey prefabricated assault tower, probably about 250 ft high, is shown in an engraving in Perrault's edition of Vitruvius's *De Architectura*.

The use of iron structures for bridges and buildings, which began a century earlier than the advent of skyscrapers with the building of the iron bridge over the River Severn in England, might have been expected to lead Europe into developing taller structures, but this was not the case because there was no economic pressure to do so, and, indeed, positive opposition to high structures. London, for example, had a limit of 80 ft from 1894 until well into the twentieth century.

Gustave Eiffel was an engineer, not an architect, and his dynamic and thrusting tower for the Paris Exhibition of 1889, which took just seventeen months to build, was put up as a temporary attraction, not as a useful building. It was a powerful demonstration of structural innovation.

However, the 985-ft tower, the tallest structure in the world until overtaken by the Chrysler Building in New York more than forty years

Family wealth and identity were displayed in the towers of San Gimignano in Tuscany, and copied in the corporate headquarters of Chicago centuries later (see opposite).

Downtown Chicago.

I saw through my window the Eiffel Tower like a flask of clear water, the domes of the Invalides and the Pantheon as a teapot and sugar basin, and the Sacré Cœur a pink and white sugarplum. Delauney came almost every day to visit me. He was always haunted by the tower.

BLAISE CENDRARS

the poet, on the Parisian painter, Robert Delauney, *Aujourd'hui*

later, changed people's perception of the world around them. First, it gave a view previously available only to hot air balloonists. Four large double-storey glass-encased lifts ran from the ground to the first-floor platform, the height of Notre Dame. Two more ran from the terrace to the second platform, the height of the dome of St Peter's. The next two stages were by hydraulic lifts. Ascent took just 7 minutes, and 2,350 passengers could be transported to the top every hour.

Secondly, it was a new experience in structural engineering, and demonstrated the possiblities of building high. Like many major architectural developments which have followed it, it generated strong and contradictory feelings amongst the public who saw it. It especially excited artists and poets.

Blaise Cendrars, one of its supporters, remarked in 1924: 'No formula of art known up to now can pretend to give plastic resolution to the Eiffel Tower. Realism shrank it; the old laws of Italian perspective diminished it. The tower rose over Paris, slender as a hat pin.' ['Plastic' is used here in its original sense of 'capable of moulding formless matter' – i.e. Cendrars felt that no existing artistic rules could have governed

Gustave Eiffel (1832–1923), the engineer who created for the Paris Exhibition of 1889, the 'temporary' tower which immortalised him.

The skyscraper, which was such a prominent feature of American architecture from the 1920s onwards, was the precocious, and occasionally delinquent, child of four grandparents: steel-framed construction, the invention of the electric elevator, high city land values and competitive advertising. The last must be included because some of the most ambitious skyscrapers have hardly been economic as buildings, but have become so because of the commercial value of a company headquarters that visibly outreaches its neighbours.
JOHN JULIUS NORWICH
General Editor
Great Architecture of the World (1975)

The Eiffel Tower in Paris, at 985 ft the world's tallest structure until the Chrysler Building in New York more than 40 years later.

The Eiffel Tower under construction. It took seventeen months to build.

The question whether the skyscraper originated in New York or Chicago is still a matter of controversy, for the answer depends on whether we define it in terms of size and economic function or in terms of structural and architectural character. If we think of the skyscraper as a high commercial building whose height greatly exceeds its horizontal dimensions and which grew out of economic exigencies arising from intensive land use, then the form may be regarded as the creation of New York builders. On the other hand, if we hold that the structural system of wind-braced steel or concrete framing expressed in an organic architectural form is an essential characteristic, then the skyscraper was a Chicago achievement. Indeed, the structural techniques used by the New York builders were for many years thoroughly conservative and lagged well behind the level reached in Chicago.
CARL J. CONDIT (1968)
quoted in
Works of Man
by Ronald W. Clark
(1985)

the shape of the Eiffel Tower.]

Others were horrified by its rude intrusion. Guy de Maupassant wrote shortly before his death: 'I left Paris and even France because of the Eiffel Tower . . . an unavoidable and tormenting nightmare.' William Morris spent two weeks gazing across the city from the Eiffel Tower's first platform because it was the only place from which the wretched Tower could not be seen!

Originally intended as a temporary structure for the Great Exhibition, the Eiffel Tower remains today only because it has succeeded as a tourist attraction far beyond its builder's expectations. Official recognition was won in the First World War, when the French Army realised that the Tower was an ideal radio beacon.

The story of high buildings intended for long-term commercial use had begun twenty years earlier in New York. What is generally taken to be the first skyscraper is the Equitable Life Assurance Building in New

The Equitable Life Assurance Building in New York, completed in 1870, was twice the height of its immediate neighbours and the first commercial office block with a passenger lift. Note the scale of the people.

A practical architect might not unnaturally conceive the idea of erecting a vast edifice whose frame should be entirely of iron . . . preserving (the frame) by means of a casing of stone.
EUGÈNE-EMMANUEL VIOLLET-LE-DUC
Lectures on Architecture,
Vol. II (*c.*1870)

Manhattan, great unfilleted sole spread out on a rock.
LE CORBUSIER

The thing generally raised on city land is taxes.
CHARLES DUDLEY WARNER
'Sixteenth Week'
My Summer in a Garden (1871)

If the owner of a skyscraper could increase his income 10 per cent, he would willingly pay half the increase just to know how. The reason why he owns a skyscraper is that science has proved that certain materials, used in a given way, can save space and increase rental incomes. A building thirty storeys high needs no more ground space than one five storeys high. Getting along with the old-style architecture costs the five-storey man the income of twenty-five floors.
HENRY FORD
(1922)

Right: Chicago was just a 'flat, low poorly drained, marshy prairie' beside Lake Michigan when Captain John Whistler built a fort there in 1803. Centre left is the John Hancock Center.

York, finished in 1870. At 130 ft, with 7 storeys, it was twice the height of its immediate neighbours; it was one of the first office blocks to have a passenger lift. It did not have the steel frame later to be a prerequisite for skyscrapers, although, curiously, Frenchman Eugène-Emmanuel Viollet-le-Duc proposed iron-skeleton buildings in his book *Lectures on Architecture* published the same year. Paris had restrictions on building height even before London but Manhattan was the ideal place for skyscrapers to take root: a raft of rock, 2½ miles wide by 18 miles long, and no legal constraints.

Between 1796 and 1811, the Commissioner's Plan was drawn up, a ruthless grid of 155 city blocks, each 200 ft long by 100 ft deep with Streets 65 ft wide running east–west between the Hudson and East Rivers, and 12 Avenues 100 ft wide. Topography was ignored. As the surveyor Kasimir Goeck so rightly predicted, this indeed was 'the best way to buy and sell real estate'. As the financial centre boomed, there was no place to go but up. Central Park, covering 840 acres and opened in 1857, was the one concession: 'The lung, the redemption and the pride of the City,' as William Cullen Bryant, Editor of the *New Evening Post* and the park's proposer, so aptly put it.

Chicago, by contrast, was a 'flat, low, poorly drained, marshy prairie', as Captain John Whistler discovered when he was ordered to build a fort at the mouth of the Checagou River in 1803. However, its

key location at the foot of Lake Michigan ensured a permanent settlement there by 1833. By the middle of the nineteenth century, Chicago had grown from a mere 300 to 650,000. By 1914 *Commerce Magazine* could record of Chicago that : 'every 40 seconds an immigrant arrives; every 6 minutes a child is born; every 7 minutes there is a funeral; every 13 minutes a couple is married; every 42 minutes a new firm starts in business'. In just 7 years, Chicago had become the fourth largest city in the world.

But back in 1871 a fire ravaged the commercial district. With characteristic energy, Chicago set about rebuilding the area. The fire prompted architects to pursue new ideas and techniques, which produced the first generation of Chicago's skyscrapers. The five- and six-storey buildings were quickly replaced with more of the same, but the Home Insurance Company commissioned William le Baron Jenney to design a new fireproof headquarters. Jenney, an engineer during the American Civil War, had used cast-iron columns in his design for the Leiter Building, although the external ones were sheathed in brick piers, and the horizontals were of timber. The 7-storey building had storey-height windows.

Armed with this experience, Jenney designed the Home Insurance Building as an iron-frame structure. It is said that Jenney stumbled on the idea of the frame when the screeching of his family parrot provoked him into slamming down a heavy book onto its steel-wire cage, and to his surprise the wire was neither bent nor cracked. The Home Insurance building had cast-iron columns and wrought-iron I-section beams, bolted together with angle brackets, which took all loads, including the external walls. The frame method allowed not only floor-to-ceiling glazing, but also faster construction, easier layouts, and a saving of as much as 10 per cent on the unusable floor area otherwise given over to structural walls.

Jenney has been criticised for not making his method of construction obviously visible to the onlooker. That charge could not be levelled at William Holabird and Martin Roche, who designed the Tacoma building of 1887. This 12-storey structure, built entirely in steel, was in sharp contrast to Burnham and Root's heavy and sullen Monadnock Building of 1891, whose 16 storeys were supported by walls 6 ft thick at ground-floor level. This was the last high building to be constructed in solid masonry, although one of the first without a trace of exterior decoration.

But in the 15-storey Reliance building three years later, Burnham summed up the spirit of the Chicago School of Architecture. Slender piers and mullions, and narrow spandrel panels in cream-coloured terracotta, separated the windows, which followed the now-familiar pattern of a large central pane of glass bounded on either side by tall, slim, opening windows. Bay windows were also used to bring in the maximum amount of light, necessary in the deep-plan (40-ft) offices.

Structure found its cleanest expression in Louis Sullivan's Carson,

The frame has been the catalyst of an architecture, but one might notice that it has also become architecture, that contemporary architecture is almost inconceivable in its absence.
COLIN ROWE
'Chicago Frame –
Chicago's Place in the Modern Movement'
Architectural Review (November 1966)

Above: Daniel H. Burnham.
Below: John W. Root.

Louis H. Sullivan.

The architects of this land and generation are now brought face to face with something new under the sun – namely that evolution and integration of social conditions, that special grouping of them, that results in a demand for the erection of tall office buildings. . .

Problem: How shall we impart to this sterile pile, this crude, harsh, brutal agglomeration, this stark, staring exclamation of eternal strife, the graciousness of those higher forms of sensibility and culture that rest on the lower and fiercer passions? How shall we proclaim from the dizzy height of this strange, weird modern housetop the peaceful evangel of sentiment, of beauty, the cult of a higher life?

LOUIS SULLIVAN
Chicago architect (1896)

The world's first skyscraper with an iron frame: Jenney's Home Insurance Building in Chicago, 1885.

Pirie & Scott Store of 1904. Although there is a proliferation of ornament around the entrance and the first and second floors, the rest of the elevations are executed in horizontal bands of windows, each framed by a moulding, which gives a fresh, streamlined appearance.

In 1896, Sullivan remarked that a tall building should be 'every inch a proud and soaring thing, rising in sheer exultation that from bottom to top as a unit without a single dissenting line'. This tenet had been clearly expressed in his earlier, perhaps more prophetic, Guaranty (now Prudential) Building in Buffalo, completed in 1895, which expresses verticality, and in which the base, shaft and capital (cornice) are clearly defined. Sullivan used the simple device of recessing the spandrels from the face of the piers to achieve this effect, reinforcing this by terminating the piers in arches beneath round windows.

The Woolworth Building has 29 lifts capable of carrying 6,000 people per hour.

The simple power of necessity is to a certain degree a principle of beauty; and these structures so plainly manifest this necessity that you feel a strange emotion in contemplating them.
PAUL BOURGET
Outremer (1895)

What is the chief feature of an office building? At once we answer, it is tall, it is lofty. It must be tall, every inch of it tall . . . it must be a proud and soaring thing, rising in sheer exultation from top to bottom without a single dissenting line.
LOUIS SULLIVAN
(1896)

The lift went into production. One of the first was installed in a 5-storey department store in the City of New York. Another design, the 'vertical screw railway', was installed in the 6-storey Fifth Avenue Hotel two years later, in 1859. The high-speed lift followed in 1879, as hydraulics replaced steam; Otis's electric lift came in 1889; push-button control followed in 1894. Double-decker lifts, similar to those used in the Eiffel Tower, were re-introduced in the 1930s; electronic controls came in 1948, and automatic doors in 1950.

The problem of vertical movement had been solved. As much care was lavished on the interior of the cars as on furnishings generally during this golden age of the skyscraper, from the turn of the century

Land is about the only thing that can't fly away.
ANTHONY TROLLOPE

The Chicago activity in erecting high buildings [of solid masonry] finally attracted the attention the local sales managers of Eastern rolling mills.
LOUIS SULLIVAN
(1895)

until the outbreak of the Second World War. Each panelled cab of the Chrysler Building lifts, for example, was finished in a different pattern of wood inlay, and those in the Woolworth Building continued the Gothic extravagance of the exterior.

There is a limit to the speed at which passengers can travel and still feel comfortable, but the taller a building becomes, the more elevators are needed to service it. They take up valuable otherwise rent-earning space. This was overcome in the Woolworth Building by having 2 of its 29 lifts carry passengers non-stop to the 54th floor, then the longest uninterrupted rise of any in the world. This idea reached its logical conclusion at the twin-towered World Trade Center in New York (1977) and in many subsequent buildings, where express cars take passengers to zone 'sky lobbies', where they transfer to lifts which provide a local service to a small number of floors.

Several other technical innovations were vital to the development of the skyscraper. Electric light made the building usable after the hours of daylight and allowed efficient use of deeper-plan floors. The telephone avoided the necessity of employing armies of messengers to carry papers between floors.

Air entering at ground level entrances turned lift and ventilation shafts into vertical wind tunnels. Debris would fly in off the street, and

Blowing machinery, an early forerunner of air conditioning, being demonstrated at the Philadelphia Centennial Exposition in 1876.

Architects and city fathers would be surprised at the amount of public concern over a city's skyline.
ADA LOUISE HUXTABLE
Kicked a Building Lately? (1976)

I've always been for grandeur . . . The history of architecture is the history of monuments. I don't think man lives by bread and bad housing alone.
PHILIP JOHNSON
(1984)

John Corpin, 'Like an ocean steamer with all Broadway in tow'.

The relentless urge to reach for the sky continued with the 1904 Times (subsequently renamed Allied Chemical) Building, the 1908 Singer Building of 47 storeys and 621 ft, and a 1909 Metropolitan Life Insurance Building, modelled on the Campanile in St Mark's Square, Venice, but more than twice its size at 700 ft.

By 1913, it in turn had been replaced as New York's tallest building by the 60-storey Woolworth, designed by Cass Gilbert, and its cost of $13.5 million paid for out of Frank W. Woolworth's own pocket. The opening of this spectacular building is described in *Corporate Design: the Interior Design and Architecture of Corporate America,* published in 1983:

'On the mild and moonless evening of 24th April 1913, thousands of spectators gathered at New York's City Hall Park as a procession of carriages and limousines entered the financial district, destined for Broadway and Park Place. There, some 900 men prominent in business, government, the arts and sciences were ushered into an improvised banquet hall on the building's 27th floor. At 7.30, the lights of the building were lowered. President Woodrow Wilson pressed a button in the White House in Washington; 80,000 lights surged on, and America's latest architectural achievement – a Gothic skyscraper, and the world's tallest building – stood out like a burning sword against the evening sky. As the crowd roared, Samuel Parkes Cadman, a prominent clergyman with a fondness for rhetoric, cried out "The Cathedral of Commerce!".'

Inspired, it is said, by the Houses of Parliament in London, the Woolworth Building was indeed the Cathedral of Commerce. Gargoyles on the lobby ceiling depict, amongst other scenes, Woolworth counting out the 5 and 10 cents made from his six hundred stores in America, Canada and England.

The Woolworth Company issued a brochure which boasted of the building's impressive features: offices for 14,000 workers, and electricity generating plants sufficient to supply a town of 50,000 population; the fastest lifts in the world; 2,800 telephones. From its 58th-floor observation platform one could see an area inhabited by 9.5 million people.

While some skyscrapers undoubtedly had aesthetic value, their prime purpose was to serve commerce. Greed, competition, and fiscal ambition ruled out concern with the environment. Consequently, by the early years of the twentieth century, New York was in danger of being choked as more and more high buildings led to canyon-like streets which severely restricted daylight and clean air. Zoning laws were introduced in 1916, creating imaginary envelopes defining both vertically and horizontally the area which could be developed. This resulted in the stepped profiles which have become so familiar.

The evident feasibility of large skyscrapers led to some ambitious proposals. In 1906, the builder Theodore Starrett proposed a 100-

'Like an ocean steamer with all Broadway in tow': the Fuller Building in New York, nicknamed the Flat Iron because of its triangular site.

storey slab-like tower divided into four zones: industry at the bottom, business in the next, residential in the next, and a hotel in the fourth. At the 20th floor there would be a market; at the 40th, a cluster of theatres, at the 60th, a shopping district, and the 80th would be the hotel's ground floor. On the roof, for good measure, there would be an amusement park, roof garden and swimming pool. The climate throughout the building would be controlled, so that people would, he claimed, have 'no need to go to Florida in the winter or Canada in the summer'. Such was the scale of this ambitious project that no one took Starrett too seriously; yet with the completion of the Empire State Building in 1931, built for 15,000 workers, and the Rockefeller Center of 1939, comprising 18 buildings from 6 to 70 storeys, such a prospect would perhaps not seem so fanciful.

The Chicago Tribune Competition of 1922, which had offered prizes totalling $100,000 for designs for 'one of the most beautiful buildings in the world', attracted 189 entries, including 54 from abroad. It was won by Raymond Hood and John Mead Howells with a Gothic Revival scheme of spiky columns culminating in a profusion of flying buttresses. Among the unsuccessful entries were such diverse proposals as a stepped cliff face (Saarinen of Finland), imitations of Giotto's Campanile in Florence, International Style (from Walter Gropius), truncated pylons, all manner of quasi-classical offerings, and jokes (well, one presumes so) for towers in the form of a giant column (Adolph Loos) and a Red Indian with a tomahawk.

The brief given to the architects for what became the most famous skyscraper of them all, however, could not have been more concise: 'A fixed budget, no space more than 28 feet from window to corridor, as many storeys in as much space as possible, an exterior of limestone, and completion by May 1931, which meant a year and six months from the beginning of the sketches'. At 1,250 ft, the Empire State building left its competitors for the 'tallest' title in the shadows of its storeys. The cost was $60 million. Jacob Raskob had a controlling interest in General Motors, and, with finance from the du Pont Company and with former democratic presidential candidate Alfred E. Smith as 'front man', proposed a major new office building. The 'Empire State' Company was named after New York State. A rivalry with the Chrysler Building undoubtedly contributed to the building's size; since Smith had lost the presidential race, he was spurred to enter one that he could – with all his financial muscle – have a chance of winning.

Demolition of the old Waldorf Astoria Hotel, to clear the site, began in October 1929. The 24th of that month saw the Wall Street Crash – but so much money had already been invested that to cancel would have meant certain loss. The Company determined to go ahead and give themselves at least a chance of eventual profit. Nevertheless, much of the building did remain unlet until the outbreak of the War – some wags suggested it should be called the 'Empty' State Building.

The skeleton of 57,000 tons of steel was completed in just 23 weeks,

The city's skyline is a physical representation of its facts of life. But a skyline is also a potential work of art.
PAUL SPREIREGEN
Urban Design (1965)

Stone by stone we shall remove the Alhambra, the Kremlin and the Louvre and build them anew on the banks of the Hudson.
BENJAMIN DE CASSERES
Mirrors of New York (1925)

I am business.
I am Profit and Loss.
I am Beauty come into the Hell of the Practical.
BENJAMIN DE CASSERES
Mirrors of New York (1925)

We in New York celebrate the black mass of Materialism.
BENJAMIN DE CASSERES
Mirrors of New York (1925)

The steel skeleton of the Empire State Building went up in 23 weeks. Each day 3,000 tradesmen worked on site to complete it just eighteen months after it was conceived.

and 3,000 tradesmen laboured daily on the site to get it finished on time. It still holds the record for the fastest skyscraper every built: at one stage it rose 14 storeys in 10 days.

The steel frame proved remarkably resilient: it survived a B25 bomber (12 tons) crashing into its side between the 78th and 79th floors in 1945 (although repairs cost more than a million dollars), and batterings from 110-mph winds and repeated lightning strikes (it was once hit 9 times in 20 minutes, but the steel frame conducted safely to earth).

When the 110-storey World Trade Center's twin towers usurped its position in the high buildings league in 1977, surpassing the New York Empire State's 46-year-old record by 100 ft, there were plans to add another 20 storeys to the original structure in retaliation; this never came to fruition.

Although the Empire State may be the world's most famous skyscraper, the Chrysler building and Rockefeller Center deserved to be more appreciated; the former for its optimism and decorative treatment as a corporate symbol, the latter for breadth and scale of planning.

Chrysler's architect was William Van Alen, who was determined – like his client – to build the tallest skyscraper come what may. The height announced for the new building was 925 ft. But 40 Wall Street, headquarters of the Bank of The Manhattan Company, was due to pip it into second place by a mere 2 ft. A spire was secretly assembled within the stainless steel sunburst motif at the Chrysler's head, and erected at the last minute as a final gesture of defiance to Van Alen's former partner, H. Craig Severance, who was architect to the Bank. Final score: 1,046 ft to 927 ft.

Inside, the entrance lobby is lined with African marble and chrome steel – somewhat theatrical and showy, perhaps, but executed with such conviction that the whole idiosyncratic structure constantly surprises and excites, without going completely over the top.

Opposite: Trump Tower, Manhattan. The saw-toothed tinted-glass façade of the Trump Tower in Manhattan conceals within it a six-storey atrium with shops, cafés, and a waterfall cascading down one wall (see photograph, p. 37). It is linked to the neighbouring greenhouse of the IBM Building, filled with bamboo plants, tables and chairs, a gift to the city in exchange for adding a few storeys of offices to its height.

In colonial days the accents of skylines proclaimed an hierarchy of values. Characteristically, the skyline consisted of church steeples at a high point with a domed building, usually a seat of government, as the focus. Fire watch towers, shot towers, or signal towers had distinct profiles and did not add confusion – neither did a cluster of ships' masts in the harbor, for they were thin, almost lacelike. All of these secondary skyline features had secondary visual roles which complemented the one or two prime skyline accents. Our contemporary skylines cannot be read in such a simple way.
PAUL SPREIREGEN
Urban Design (1965)

Give me your tired, your poor,
Your huddled masses yearning to be free:
The wretched refuse of your teeming shore
Send these, the homeless, tempest-tossed
*   to me.*
Poem by
EMMA LAZARUS
at the Statue of Liberty,
welcoming immigrants to the New World.

Architects dressed as their buildings for the Beaux-Arts Ball, held at the Hotel Astor, New York, on 23 January 1931. In the centre is William Van Alen as the Chrysler Building.

Opposite and *right*: Chrysler Building, New York. The famous sunburst motif of the Chrysler Building in Manhattan crowns the 1,046-ft skyscraper. It was designed by William Van Alen, whose client, Walter Chrysler, said: 'Make this building higher than the Eiffel Tower,' which he did in 1930. The following year it was beaten into second place as the world's tallest by the Empire State Building. The building is decorated with the car firm's chevron logo, a frieze of car wheels with silver hub caps and crowned with rainbow ribbons of roof.

Oh, blank confusion! true epitome
Of what the mighty city is herself,
To thousands upon thousands of her
*   sons,*
Living amid the same perpetual whirl
Of trivial objects, melted and reduced
To one identity, by differences
That have no law, no meaning, and no
*   end –*
WILLIAM WORDSWORTH
Prelude, Book VIII

In matters of grave importance, style,
not sincerity, is the vital thing.
OSCAR WILDE
The Importance of Being Earnest

In architecture? CK

strokes of his pen, as it were, Mies laid the foundation for all the great steel-and-glass skyscrapers we see around us today.'

The finest of them all is the Seagram Building of 1958 in New York, rising 58 storeys above Park Avenue. Nicknamed the 'Bronze Baby', its exterior is a series of parallel bronze I-beams running the full height of the building, interspersed with brown-tinted glass. Philip Johnson, Mies's assistant, said of it, 'He tried to make beauty out of the bones.' Mies himself said, 'Less is more.' The design was Cartesian geometry as an expression of the industrial age, relying on precise engineering and subtlety of proportion for its effect. A few years earlier, Mies's most devoted followers, the Chicago firm of Skidmore, Owings and Merrill, had completed Lever House for the soap company. It comprises two curtain-walled blocks, like two cigar boxes. The vertical one sits upon the other, which is horizontal. Both are freed from the ground on *piloti* (stilts). The term 'curtain-walled' means that the walls are nonstructural, made of glass in a metal frame. The sophistication of Seagram or Lever has never been equalled since, in spite of numerous attempts to emulate them.

New York – 'where style is confused with substance, glamour mistaken for beauty and what you wear matters more than what you are'.
SHIRLEY LOWE
in a profile of the author Jay McInerney
The Times (8 February 1985)

The 'Bronze Baby', Mies van der Rohe and Philip Johnson's Seagram Building in New York. Mies said, 'Less is more'; Johnson said, 'He tried to make beauty out of the bones.'

Overleaf: Cartoons of the proposed Mansion House Square office block, London, designed by Mies van der Rohe in the mid 1960s, and refused planning permission in 1985 after a public inquiry. Patrick Jenkin, the former Environment Secretary, is performing his swansong as King Kong.

SOM's John Hancock Center, Chicago, designed by Bruce Graham. Diagonal bracing gives it a unique public face.

SOM were dubbed 'The Three Blind Mies' by Frank Lloyd Wright. He was referring to their adoption of Miesian approaches to almost every building type. Under the direction of Bruce Graham, SOM became one of the most innovative in the use of structural systems for skyscrapers. The two most important ones are both in Chicago: the John Hancock Center (95 storeys) and the Sears Tower (1,454 ft and 110 storeys, the tallest building in the world).

The John Hancock Center, often referred to as Big John or The Gallows, has a range of uses on different levels – offices, flats, restaurants, an observation floor, a swimming pool on the 44th floor. It is of hull-and-core construction: the core of lifts and services provides a strong structural resistance to wind loads; the hull is formed by the exterior walls, in this case regularly spaced exterior columns interconnected with diagonal and horizontal members, acting as a rigid box like a bridge. A similar hull-and-core construction, though without the diagonal bracing, was used by Graham in the Sears Tower. Nine square tubes nestling together extend to different heights, giving it a stepped profile (see p. 201).

The introduction of high-strength steel has enabled much more efficient structures to be built. For example, the World Trade Center in New York, with twin towers rising 110 storeys to 1,350 ft, uses only as much steel as the Chrysler Building, but is a third higher. The John Hancock Center uses only 70 per cent of the steel that was needed in the Empire State Building. Wind conditions created by the Hancock building were largely responsible for the decision to build the neighbouring Water Tower Place, 76 storeys and 859 ft, in reinforced concrete, the world's tallest building in this method of construction.

The post-war period of skyscraper design has also been characterised by the use of huge areas of glazing in place of the terracotta or stone of pre-war examples. Mies van der Rohe's influential drawings of glass-encased towers finally saw fulfilment at Lake Shore Drive, Chicago, in 1949. In two 26-storey towers of flats, the architect first used I-section black steel plate, in this case to hide fireproof concrete casings to the steel structure which would otherwise mar the pure lines of the design. It was the start of a new Chicago aesthetic of glass skins, an idea which again travelled far afield. Since the 1950s the glass has often been tinted, mirrored, or used in double-glazed units to reduce glare, heat loss and solar heat gain. The sheer undulating walls of the Lake Point Tower apartment building in Chicago took glass to the 645-ft height of the tower. It was designed by two architects who had studied under Mies, and then advanced his half-a-century-old dream.

There were also some spectacular failures of new glazing technology, as in the John Hancock Tower in Boston, where some of the 10,000 double-glazed insulating sandwiches fell off the building. They were replaced with painted plywood. This and other skyscraper disaster stories form a chapter in Peter Blake's *Form Follows Fiasco*.

The International Style architecture of the post-war years was the

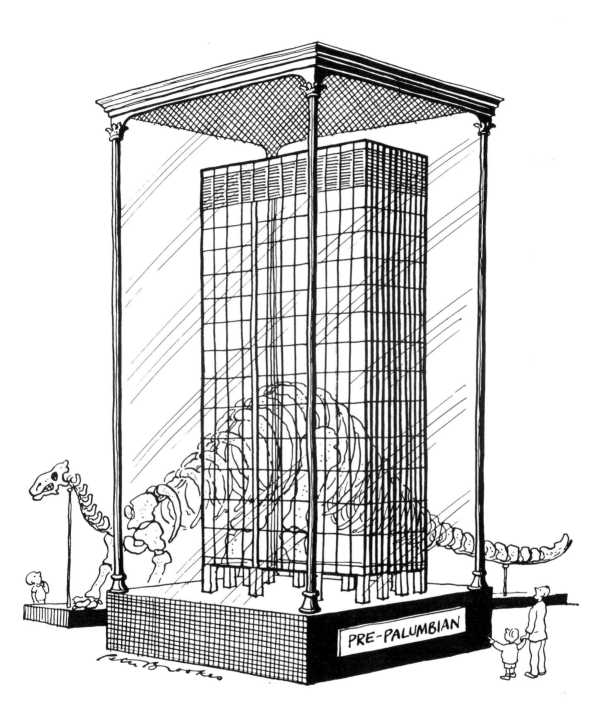

PRE-PALUMBIAN

The forest of towers which is Manhattan Island today. On the left is the Empire State Building, at 1,250 ft New York's tallest until the World Trade Center usurped the title in 1977.

For architects just happen to be the handmaidens of the speculators who work toward 'the death of the city by development'. The phrase is Ada Louise Huxtable's, New York's guardian angel without portfolio, and architecture critic of the Times. Are the harsh words justifiable? Or could it be that we are misreading the profoundest thoughts of those architects who give aid and comfort (in the form of drawings and specifications) to the vilest schemes of the developers? Architects probably have known all along that the demise of American cities is inevitable, and content themselves with practising urban euthenasia. At all events, their callous kiss of death pays off handsomely. 'Human amenties? Urban aesthetics? Public good?' asks Mrs Huxtable. 'None of it balances against private profit.'
BERNARD RUDOFSKY
Streets for People:
A Primer for Americans (1969)

third phase of expression used by the designers of America's sky-scrapers, a development from the Renaissance palazzi and Gothic Revival structures of its two previous manifestations in Chicago and New York. But with hindsight one can see inevitable reaction against this latest style; and it was Philip Johnson, Mies's chief acolyte and propagandist, who led it. 'He believed in the ultimate truth of architecture, and especially of his architecture,' Johnson recalled of Mies later. 'He thought it was closer to the truth, capital T, than anyone else's because it was simpler, and could be learned, adapted on and on into the centuries. In a way this was bad because it gave everyone a licence – *I am doing Mies!* Every architect could say to his client, 'I can do a building cheaper than I did for you last year, because now I have religion! – flat roof, factory-made curtain walls, a rationalization for cheapness.'

The first of the new breed was Johnson's AT & T headquarters building in New York, unveiled in 1978, a pink-granite tower sandwiched between some Renaissance historicism from one source (a church by

Postwar architecture is the accountants' revenge on the prewar businessmen's dreams.
REM KOOLHAAS
Delirious New York (1978)

The John Hancock Tower in Boston, after it had shed many of its 10,000 windows. The black areas are painted plywood.

By 1980, one thing was clear: the box, the rationalist dream of the International Style, was making more and more architects uncomfortable. Not only was it no longer the clean and exhilarating structure that would serve as a clarion call to a new age, but it was not even able to hold out much promise of practicality. It was generally inefficient from the standpoint of energy, and it was not as marketable from the viewpoint of real estate operators either.
PAUL GOLDBERGER
The Skyscraper (1982)

Architecture is very much like the oldest profession in the world: it has only one aim, and that is to please for a fee.
PHILIP JOHNSON
(1984)

We're having a lot of fun. Now you can say it's much better to build higher buildings for the greater glory of God than it is for the greater glory of Mammon, but that isn't what we think now.
PHILIP JOHNSON
(1984)

Alberti) at its base, and a furniture-style (Chippendale highboy) broken pediment at its peak. Now Johnson uses virtually any style of packaging to give corporate identity and disguise square footage, from the Gothic in glass spires of his Pittsburgh Plate Glass Company headquarters in Pittsburgh (see p. 166) to residential blocks which look like crenellated castles or French Empire mansions.

Johnson's break with orthodoxy has led to a free-for-all among other architects in terms of stylistic expression: Helmut Jahn, Kohn Pedersen Fox, Cesar Pelli, and Michael Graves are among those exploring new eclectic territory in search of convincing styles. But the current situation does beg the question whether what they are doing is really architecture and not mere window-dressing.

Zoning laws were changed in New York in 1961 to allow the erection of skyscrapers which went straight up from the street, rather then set back; densities in the Big Apple have been allowed as never before. Between 1980 and 1983, 30 skyscrapers were started or completed in

Philip Johnson's AT&T building in New York: corporate identity based on the Chippendale highboy.

Interviewer: *How do you think Mies might regard AT & T?*
Philip Johnson: *I think he would be absolutely horrified.*

[Today's] buildings are not architecture, but packaging glued together with epoxy or neoprene . . . It is all a technological funfair of the shifty age of make-believe, high turnover, low-profile, cover operations and massage parlours. Indeed, as could be expected, our art reflects vividly a demented society that has had its day.
BERTHOLD LUBETKIN
RIBA President's invitation lecture (1985)

Architecture can never be produced by men that have lost the power to wonder.
RALPH TUBBS
The Englishman Builds (1945)

The only real advantage of New York is that all its inhabitants ascend to heaven right after their deaths, having served their full term in hell right on Manhattan Island.
Barnard Bulletin
(22 September 1967)

Skyscrapers – mountains for people to climb.
BRUCE GRAHAM
(1984)

mid-town Manhattan, containing 14 million sq. ft of space – the equivalent of 70 Centre Points! 'At this level of over-building,' remarked Ada Louise Huxtable (former architecture critic of the *New York Times*), 'aesthetics cancel out. Architects are having a wonderful time rearranging deck-chairs on the *Titanic.*'

There are few skyscrapers outside Chicago or New York which demand much attention; fewer still outside America. Among the exceptions are the regional references of the Torre Velasca and the elegance and innovation of the Pirelli building, both in Milan. Few places can claim restricted land and rocketing land values as an excuse for building so tall, and if they do, then excellence is not usually a criterion for design. Hong Kong, however, does have good reason to reach for the sky; and with the completion in 1985 of British architect Norman Foster's headquarters for the Hongkong and Shanghai Banking Corporation, this part of south-east Asia has made a distinguished contribution to the history of the form. The steel cathedral for the high priests of banking, 47 storeys high and costing almost £500 million, was designed as a prefabricated kit

It is well worthwhile to invest an extra 10 per cent in the construction of an office building with a more marketable presence.

GERALD D. HINES

New York property developer, on the value of architecture as corporate identity

The skyscraper is the miracle and monument of the twentieth century.

ADA LOUISE HUXTABLE

(Architecture Critic *New York Times*)

of parts, with 100 sub-contractors in 80 countries around the world supplying components which were then slotted together on site. The reason was partly speed of construction, partly quality control. Like the John Hancock Center in Chicago, bridge-building technology was applied to the design of the structure; eight steel masts suspend the floors of 100-ft clear span (for flexibility), and 139 modules of services (including lavatories, electrical and mechanical plant) were 'plugged in' at two sides to feed in elements more commonly found in a central core.

Apart from its structural virtuosity, clearly visible as one looks across the water from Kowloon, visitors are spellbound by the 170-ft high banking hall, a dynamic space with double-height escalators shooting up through a glazed floor screen, and the light flooding the space, beamed down from a 'sunscoop' and reflectors at the top. The building has a level of sophistication at present unmatched by any of its rivals, even though it is far from being the tallest architecture in the world.

The banking hall of Norman Foster's Hongkong and Shanghai Banking Corporation headquarters , Hong Kong, at the opening of the first phase in July 1985.

The growing sophistication in the control of environment systems in skyscrapers is the most significant new development in the closing decades of the twentieth century. The 'smart' or 'intelligent' building is one with computer-controlled automated lighting systems, talking lifts, and heat and motion sensors, shared by tenants of the building for an increased annual rental charge per square foot. Shared tenant services was an idea born with the deregulation of the American telephone industry, and uses sophisticated wiring and digital telephone switching systems.

City Place, a 38-storey tower in Hartford, Connecticut, was one of the first of the dozen or so 'smart' buildings now in operation. A computer voice announces each floor in the lift, and there are no light switches in the offices: instead, an infra-red scanner which senses body heat and motion turns the lights on as soon as someone enters a room and off again 12 minutes after the last person leaves. Changes in temperature as small as one-tenth of a degree adjust the heating, cooling and humidity in each room. In a fire the alarm system notifies the fire department, alerts occupants to evacuate, sends lifts to appropriate positions and raises air pressure in the floors immediately above and below the outbreak to prevent the fire spreading.

Tenants get their phone and computer services from the building owner, giving small companies telecommunication and data-processing facilities usually available only to large companies.

But height remains the ultimate measure of a skyscraper. The old rivalry between New York and Chicago is sure to continue in the title bid for 'world's tallest building'. Early in 1985, three schemes were submitted for New York's Coliseum site which would have been the tallest if built: a 137-storey tower by Eli Attia and Associates, a 135-storey tower by Helmut Jahn, and one of similar height by Skidmore, Owings and Merrill. SOM also undertook a study for a 170-storey Chicago World Trade Center, half a mile high, which would have 2.2 million sq. ft of residential space, a 2,400 room hotel, 750,000 sq. ft of offices, more than 1.5 million sq. ft of exhibition space, parking for 4,000 cars, and 500,000 sq. ft of retail space. SOM's Bruce Graham has remarked, however, that the economics of such a structure defeated the objective, as the interest repayments over the time it would take to construct the building would be greater than its earnings. Even so, another Chicago architect, Harry Weese, drew up an alternative scheme, 210 storeys, and 2,500 ft high, which would cost $2,000 million.

Such an idea may seem fanciful today, some 60 years after Le Corbusier proposed his city for three million people housed in a forest of tall blocks, and 30 years since Frank Lloyd Wright unveiled his plans for a mile-high skyscraper of 528 storeys. Only Paolo Soleri's 'arcologies', which are discussed later, have gone further.

But the final word on the hundred-year history of this phenomenon should be left to Arthur Drexler, director of the Architecture Department of the Museum of Modern Art in New York: 'Skyscrapers are machines for making money. They exploit land values to the point of rendering cities uninhabitable. But that's no reason to stop building them. In a free society, capitalism gives us what we want, including our own demise.'

New York is different. It is a very tight little island, not really part of the United States, it belongs to the world. It lives in an abstract world of economics and finance.
BRUCE GRAHAM
(1984)

Three contenders for the world's tallest
building were proposed for New York's
Coliseum site in 1985: (from left) SOM's
web-like structure for Sam Lefrak,
Helmut Jahn's Spiral for Donald Trump
and Elia Attia's 137-storey tower for the
same developer. None will be built.

CHAPTER THREE

HOME, SWEET CONSUMER DURABLE

*If I had to say which was telling the
truth about society, a speech by the
Minister of Housing, or the actual
buildings put up in his time, I should
believe the buildings.*
KENNETH CLARK
Civilisation (1969)

*The age we live in will surely be known
as the age of invention. This has its
dangers and its penalties, but it should
also have its rewards and excitements.
The skill and ingenuity of our
technicians can revolutionise housing as
they have revolutionised so many other
undertakings.*
ANEURIN BEVAN
Minister of Health,
in the foreword to *Homes for the People*
published by the
Association of Building Technicians
(1946).

*The house looms large, if not as a
refuge, as a metaphor, live, dead and
mixed. It is the repository of our wishes
and dreams, memories and illusions. It
is, or at least ought to be, instrumental
in the transition from being to well-
being.*
BERNARD RUDOFSKY
The Prodigious Builders (1977)

**Utopian dream turns into urban
nightmare: a tower block is demolished
using controlled explosions in Hackney,
east London.**

Until the Industrial Revolution, almost every inhabitant of Britain had
the means – either wealth or unrestricted access to natural resources –
to construct his own house. This was to change in the rapid urbanisation
which followed the growth of industrial centres, with the concomitant
need to have large work forces living near their places of work. The
rural poor set out for the factories in the belief that the prosperity of the
towns would improve their lot, but in practice the uncontrolled growth
created conditions of immense squalor; they now lacked the means to
improve their surroundings and became the first generation of the urban
industrial poor.

The new industrial barons were reluctant to acknowledge that this
new urban population had a right to a decent standard of housing.
Successive governments, perhaps misled by the overwhelmingly successful economic consequences of the new technology, saw no need to
intervene.

It was not until the efforts of individual activists like John Ruskin
(1819–1900) that any action was taken. He recognised that 'lodgements'
for working people would have to be provided through legislation, and
that the need would be beyond the capacities either of private philanthropy or the 'enlightened self-interest' economics of Adam Smith.

Ruskin also foresaw 'garden cities'. In his book *The Seven Lamps of
Architecture* of 1849, he wrote that it would be necessary to build 'more
strongly, beautifully . . . [with] clean and busy streets within, and the
open country without, with a belt of beautiful garden and orchard round
the walls, so that from any part of the city perfectly fresh air and grass
and the sight of the far horizon may be reachable in a few minutes' walk.'

In the first half of the nineteenth century, housing reform was driven
largely by the engine of voluntary effort, and a number of philanthropic
societies built experimental housing blocks for the 'respectable' urban
poor. Ruskin himself helped Octavia Hill, the social reformer, to provide

accommodation at low rent. Yet by 1875 she had to record that private benevolence still housed only 26,000 people in London, roughly equivalent to the population increase every six months (London's population had doubled from one to two million in the first fifty years of the nineteenth-century).

Long before governments accepted the need for the provision of housing as a tenet of a welfare state, royalty played a part. Queen Victoria's consort, Prince Albert, was active in promoting good housing, in his capacity as president of the Society for Improving the Condition of the Labouring Classes. The Society commissioned new houses with adequate sanitation which could be built at minimum expense. They were designed by Henry Roberts, an architect, who incorporated the latest ideas on health and the need of single men and families. Among their features were hollow bricks for better insulation and damp-proofing; hygienic finishes; water supply and internal sanitation; separate bedrooms for children of different sexes; and an emphasis on fresh air for good health. Prince Albert used his influence as President of the Commissioners of the Great Exhibition of 1851 to have a pair of Roberts' model cottages built near Hyde Park Barracks during the show. (It is ironic, given his concern with sanitary housing, that Albert should have died of typhoid.) The houses were seen by thousands, including builders and landowners. After the Exhibition the cottages were removed and rebuilt at the entrance to Kennington Park, where they are still in use today. Another pair can be found in Windsor, built by the Royal Windsor Improvement Society.

Model workers' cottages built for the Great Exhibition of 1851. Later they were rebuilt at Kennington Park where they stand today.

Small rooms or dwellings discipline the mind, large ones weaken it.
LEONARDO DA VINCI
Notebooks (c.1500)

Our houses are such unwieldy property that we are often imprisoned rather than housed in them.
HENRY DAVID THOREAU
'Economy' in *Walden*

[A man's house is] the theatre of his hospitality, the seat of his self-fruition and the comfortablest part of his own life.
SIR HENRY WOTTON
Elements of Architecture (1624)

American philanthropist George Peabody was also working to improve the housing conditions of the new city-dwellers. In Spitalfields, the most overcrowded district in east London, it was reported that one house contained 60 people, 7 to a room, with only 9 beds. In 1864, Peabody decided to build a model dwelling, five storeys high, offering three-room flats for five shillings a week, with water, sanitation and a communal laundry. He then set up the Peabody Trust, donating £500,000 for similar tenements to be built in Chelsea, Islington, Shadwell and 26 other London districts. 29 of these buildings still stand today.

The pioneering efforts of these early reformers finally provoked some government action. The Public Health Act of 1875 introduced statutory planning and servicing of towns, and a public health inspectorate which had powers to improve environmental conditions. By-laws were introduced to control new building. The building of homes,

Boundary Street flats, opened in 1895 by the newly formed London County Council. Slum clearance was followed by the construction of mansion blocks for the working class.

however, was left to the private sector until architects from London County Council, which took over from the Metropolitan Board of Works, first became involved in public housing in 1873. Architects suddenly entered the world of providing housing on a vast scale. As building controls became increasingly complex, architects were needed to administer and co-ordinate. They acquired a role in mass housing, and became independent arbiters between the client and the builder. The tenant, however, was not consulted. Public sector housing increasingly took over as the philanthropic system proved inadequate for the task.

The weakness of the Peabody Trust and similar organisations was one of finance. An acceptable rate of return required from the investment (3½ per cent or more in those days) pushed up rents to more than the lowest-paid tenants could afford. Evidence given by the London Trades Council to a Royal Commission in 1884 said: 'It is totally impossible that private enterprise, philanthropy and charity can ever keep pace with the present demands. . . . Economic forces and population have outstepped their endeavours; hence evils accrue. But what the individual cannot do, the state municipality must seek to accomplish . . . for it alone possesses the necessary power and wealth.'

Visions of what public sector housing might be like could be seen in the model settlements built by industrialists and philanthropists with Utopian ideals.

At New Lanark in Scotland, Robert Owen founded a model community based around a mill. Between 1800 and 1825, he built a school, a laundry, a co-operative grocery and a vegetable market, and homes better than any other workers could hope to have. The community was, he declared, 'a self-employing, self-supporting, self-educating and self-governing population' of about 1,800 Scots. Their lives were shaped by

London County Council housing at White Hart Lane, Tottenham, opened in 1904. Small-scale terraces and open space.

There, sighs, laments and loud wailings resounded through the starless air . . . Strange tongues, horrible cries, groans of pain, cries of anger, shrill and hoarse voices, and the sound of beatings, made a tumult, circling in the eternal darkness, like sand eddying in a whirlwind.
DANTE
Inferno, iii, 22–30

Above: Robert Owen's model community at New Lanark in Scotland. He built a school, laundry, co-operative grocery, vegetable market and homes around his mill.

Right: The school at New Lanark, part of Owen's 'self-employing, self-supporting, self-educating and self-governing' community.

regulations, temperance, cleanliness and hard work. Owen paid higher wages for shorter hours than any other industrialist, and still made a profit. New Lanark's reputation spread all over the world, prompting a visit even from Tsar Nicholas of Russia. Its success led to many similar such ventures. Later, however, he was to found the less successful Co-operative Community of New Harmony in Indiana. Here he lost all his money, returning almost penniless to Scotland.

Not long after the completion of New Lanark, Sir Titus Salt built an Italian Renaissance mill outside Bradford, designed by local architects Lockwood and Mawson, and planted around it a community in fine houses with a church, laundry, library, and almshouses. It is said that he was inspired by reading Disraeli's novel *Sybil,* which describes just such a model village built around a mill. There were others, too: notably Bournville, established by Cadbury (1839–1922), patriarch of the Quaker Chocolate Empire, and Port Sunlight, founded on the soap industry of William Hesketh Lever (1851–1925). Port Sunlight, the model settlement on the Mersey, attempted to integrate an industrial

community with village life. When the scheme was started in 1888, its founder (later the 1st Viscount Leverhulme) said: 'It is my and my brother's hope someday to build houses in which our workpeople will be able to live and be comfortable – semi-detached houses with gardens back and front in which they will be able to know more about the science of life than they can in a back-to-back slum, and in which they will learn that there is more enjoyment in life than the mere going to and returning from work and looking forward to Saturday night to draw their wages.'

The régime may have been oppressively paternalistic, allowing little independence of thought or action and demanding complete allegiance to its founder; but architecturally it was a considerable achievement. Materials and styles were employed to delight the eye, from half-timbering and turrets to patterned brickwork, arches, and stone flag roofs. Lever's architects were left to create variety and interest within an overall framework. Decoration was of a high order and no craftsmanship was spared. Good housing was for the first time not just the privilege of the few.

The achievements of Cadbury and Lever were later to be reflected in the Garden City movement. This was founded by Ebenezer Howard, a clerk from London who, after living in Chicago, returned to England with radical ideas about getting the best from town and country. His basic philosophy, set out in *Garden Cities of Tomorrow* at the turn of the century, was that, to counteract the abandonment of rural areas, and the consequent sprawl of overcrowded cities, new towns of restricted size should be built within permanent agricultural belts. Houses and workplaces were to be fully integrated, and the whole place should be retained within joint freehold ownership so that all increases in value

Port Sunlight, where William Hesketh Lever attempted to integrate an industrial community with village life.

The London Underground led to the growth of suburbia. Golders Green in 1908 was depicted in a London Transport poster.

should benefit the whole community. His book contained a drawing of the Three Magnets, demonstrating the advantages of living and working in the same place. 'Town and country *must be married,*' he wrote, 'and out of this joyous union will spring a new hope, a new life, a new civilisation.' This was planning on a grand scale – garden cities of 30,000 people.

Community ownership was intended to avoid both the paternalism of Bournville and Port Sunlight, and profiteering in land speculation and building by industrialists and entrepreneurs. A property-owning democracy and the owner–occupier had become a reality. Houses were to be built to show 'the fullest measure of individual taste and preference'.

The influence of the Garden City concept spread not only through Britain but also across America, France, Germany and Sweden. The movement was concerned more with planning than with styles of housing, but it was part of the great reforming impetus which accompanied government involvement in a range of welfare services, from the recognition of trade unions and minimum wages to the provision of free education. The Housing and Town Planning Act of 1909 required local authorities to build new homes, but it was not until the Addison Act, ten years later, that it became a significant part of government expenditure.

Before the First World War, few houses were built by public authorities: between 1890 and 1914 only 14,000 dwellings were erected, just 600 a year. Other housing was built privately, for rent. Victory in that Great War gave rise to great rhetoric, and Prime Minister Lloyd George promised 'Homes fit for Heroes' on their return from the trenches. In the 60 years from 1914 to 1974 there was a six-fold increase in owner-occupation, matching a six-fold decrease in privately rented accommodation. At the same time the public rented sector rose by some thirty-three times.

The council-house boom, which lasted until the mid 1970s, was the result of the Housing and Town Planning Act of 1919. This imposed a statutory duty on all local authorities to build their own houses with the help of government subsidies. There was an important link between this programme of public-sector housing and the earlier idealism of reformers and philanthropists such as Cadbury and Lever. Raymond Unwin, Ebenezer Howard's architect for Letchworth Garden City, became chief architect for housing and planning in the newly created Ministry of Health from the end of the War until 1928, and was largely responsible for the content of a report by Sir John Tudor-Walters which set out standards and design criteria for council estates. This report came to the conclusion that the 'self-contained cottage', rather than tenements, was the most suitable form of accommodation for the working classes. Local authorities and private developers adopted this advice, and the typical layouts of the four million houses built during the next twenty years reflected a pared-down version of the Garden City home. But very quickly Unwin's sensitive guidelines were compro-

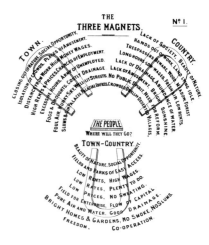

Ebenezer Howard's Three Magnets, published in his book *Garden Cities of Tomorrow* at the turn of the century.

In residential planning, and in municipal housing in particular, the social and institutional relationships are as old, and indeed older, than the provision of state housing itself. The three participants – the local authority which commissions the work, the architect who executed it, and the tenant – are in a fixed and more or less rigid relationship with one another. In origin, the tenant was a member of the urban poor, unable to pay for sanitary housing himself, and expected to be the passive recipient of the model housing provided.
ALISON RAVETZ
Architectural Research (April 1971)

Letchworth Garden City, designed by Raymond Unwin, who became chief architect for housing and planning in the Ministry of Health from the end of the First World War until 1928.

mised in the hands of borough engineers, and developments consisting almost exclusively of low-density housing for the middle classes sprang up. Slum dwellers had to wait until the mid 1930s, when they frequently ended up in new blocks of flats in the centre of towns and cities.

The Oxford Wall, built to separate a private estate from a council estate in the 1920s, indicated the antipathy which the middle class had to the idea of council housing near their properties.

The moment that housing, a universal human activity, becomes defined as a problem, a housing problems industry is born, with an army of experts, bureaucrats and researchers, whose existence is a guarantee that the problem won't go away.

COLIN WARD

in the preface to John F. C. Turner's book *Housing by People* (1976)

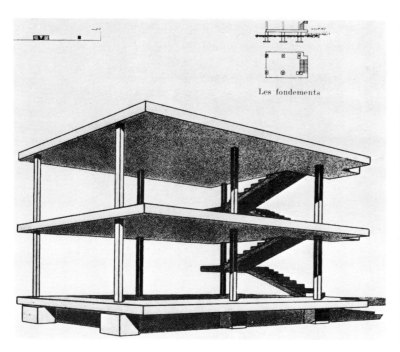

Les fondements

Le Corbusier's Domino House: 'a completely new method of construction' in reinforced concrete.

Le Corbusier.

In Europe, however, a design-led revolution was occuring. In 1914 a 27-year-old Swiss architect Charles-Édouard Jeanneret (1887–1965), who adopted the pseudonym Le Corbusier, proposed the Domino House which, he hoped, would 'result in a completely new method of construction'. It took the form of a basic shell of ground and first-floor slabs and a roof, held up by six columns, and a staircase. Windows, doors, partitions and external walls were then inserted in this structural frame. It was a powerful image, and the architect's heroic drawings were matched by a Messianic flow of words of equal potency. A few years later, he wrote:

A great epoch has begun.
There exists a new spirit.

Industry, overwhelming us like a flood which rolls on towards its destined ends, has furnished us with new tools adapted to this new epoch, animated by the new spirit.

Economic law inevitably governs our acts and our thoughts.

The problem of the house is a problem of the epoch. The equilibrium of society today depends upon it. Architecture has for its first duty, in this period of renewal, that of bringing about a revision of values, a revision of the constituent elements of the house.

Mass-production is based on analysis and experiment.

Mass Housing in its original conception was never intended to house the entire community. It was merely an emergency measure which was seized upon when the normal process fell short. It was a means which was useful when large numbers of people had to be housed in a short space of time . . . [it] has indeed been a blessing in recent times for countless people, and as an emergency measure has contributed to the fact that our civilisation has survived the industrial revolution. But our problem began when this emergency measure from the turn of the century grew into housing for the entire community, and thus became the norm.

N. J. HABRAKEN
Supports: An Alternative to Mass Housing (1972)

Methods based on craftmanship are antiquated and must be replaced by the acceptance of a modern concept of industry. The search for the odd, the wish to be different from one's neighbour, makes unity of style impossible . . . Our age, after a sad interregnum is approaching Zeitstil which will honour traditions but fight false romanticism. Objectivity and reliability are once more gaining ground.
WALTER GROPIUS
(1910)

Away with medievalism, then, and the medieval concept of handicrafts and ultimately with handicrafts themselves, as mere training and means for the purposes of form.
OSKAR SCHLEMMER
discarding the crafts approach
at the Bauhaus (1922)

Pessac was conceived to be built of reinforced concrete. The aim: low cost. The means: reinforced concrete. The method: standardization, industrialization, tailorised mass production.
LE CORBUSIER
on his housing at Cité Frugès, Pessac, near Bordeaux, completed in 1926

Given the trend of our age to eliminate the craftsman more and more, yet greater savings by means of industrialisation, can be foretold, though in our country they may for the time being still appear Utopian.
WALTER GROPIUS
to the AEG company (1910)

Industry on the grand scale must occupy itself with building and establish the elements of the house on a mass-production basis.

We must create the mass-production spirit.
The spirit of constructing mass-production houses.
The spirit of living in mass-production houses.
The spirit of conceiving mass-production houses.

If we eliminate from our hearts and minds all dead concepts in regard to the house, and look at the question from a critical and objective point of view, we shall arrive at the 'House-Machine', the mass-production house, healthy (and morally so too) and beautiful in the same way that the working tools and instruments which accompany our existence are beautiful.

Beautiful also with all the animation that the artist's sensibility can add to severe and pure functioning elements.

(*Vers une Architecture,* 1923)

Le Corbusier's arguments influenced a generation of planners, politicians and architects. Technology was to be employed to produce social reform, and architectural determinism was born: new surroundings in a universal style would create new, and it was implied, *better* people. Artistic individuality and romanticism were rejected in favour of collaborative effort and a rational approach to every problem. In Germany in the 1920s and early 1930s Gropius and his colleagues at the Bauhaus were developing an equally uncompromising but more political theory of architecture. One of the manifestos of the Novembergruppe, a forerunner of the Bauhaus which had Gropius among its members, urged action:

Painters, Architects, Sculptors, you whom the bourgeoisie pays with high rewards for your work – out of vanity, snobbery, and boredom – Hear! To this money there clings the sweat and blood and nervous energy of thousands of poor hounded human beings – Hear! It is an unclean profit . . . we must be true socialists – we must kindle the highest socialist virtue: the brotherhood of man.

Public ownership of land and the means of production were seen as a necessary condition for radical change. Model estates were built in Berlin, Frankfurt and Stuttgart. They had great expanses of white walls in pre-cast concrete, ribbon windows (bands of window uninterrupted by mullions), and flat roofs, all paying homage to the right angle.

The vertical thrust of American skyscrapers was gaining influence in Europe and Le Corbusier's 'vertical city . . . bathed in light and air' was to be adopted by virtually every industrialised nation after the Second

World War. The 'self-contained cottage' had no meaning for the new Europeans, and mass production began to dictate its own terms.

In Weimar Germany between 1924 and 1932, more than 70 per cent of all new dwellings were built in whole or in part with government money. Much of this work was carried out by Gropius and his Bauhaus colleagues – Bruno Taut, Erich Mendelsohn and Ernst May. May took over Frankfurt's municipal building and, as a devoted Communist, embarked on a social housing programme of the Siedlung or 'settlement'. The White House (Weissenhof) Siedlung of 1927 in Stuttgart was built as part of a trade fair, with Le Corbusier, Mies van de Rohe, Gropius and Taut among the designers. It was the most influential scheme of its era, a lesson in 'minimal housing', although built to a much higher standard than could be used for large-scale building.

In 1933, the Nazis closed the Bauhaus, and its members emigrated to Russia and America, though several stopped off in England before continuing their journey west. British architects such as F. R. S. Yorke had already learnt much about the birth of the Modern Movement on the Continent through the meetings of CIAM (Congrès Internationaux d'Architecture Moderne), founded five years previously, and through the MARS (Modern Architecture Research) Group, its English equivalent set up by Wells Coates and Morton Shand in 1933. In *The Modern House* (1934), Yorke remarked, as had Le Corbusier before him, that ships, cars and aeroplanes represented the new technological age. 'Twentieth-century architecture,' he wrote, 'is dictated by the new methods of construction and new materials, and by unprecedented practical requirements, a new outlook on life, a new sense of space and time. If we are to act in accordance with tradition we must allow these factors to determine the twentieth-century aesthetic.'

Wealthy patrons provided most of the commissions for the new architecture in one-off houses. Connell, Ward and Lucas, Yorke (teamed with Marcel Breuer), Peter Behrens, Wells Coates and D. Pleydell-Bouverie, Walter Gropius and Maxwell Fry were among the favoured architects. Fry's house near Kingston, completed in 1937, is a notable example.

The recent publicity surrounding Ronan Point and the very serious shortcomings of the building methods used in the construction of such blocks of flats has highlighted the errors made in the 1960s. There is no point in apportioning blame to anyone, for we know where we went wrong, but I do think it is important to remind ourselves of the philosophy which tended to lie behind the strategy and which influenced architects and planners alike.

From this point of view it is instructive to read what the late Mies van der Rohe wrote as far back as 1924. Apart from saying that 'architecture is the will of the epoch translated into space', he also said that 'we do not respect flights of the spirit as much as we value reason and realism. We are concerned today with questions of a general nature. The individual is losing significance; his destiny is no longer what interests us. The decisive achievements in all fields are impersonal and their authors are for the most part unknown. They are part of the trend of our time toward anonymity.'
HRH THE PRINCE OF WALES
addressing the
Institute of Directors' annual convention (1985)

Opposite: **The White House (Weissenhof) Siedlung, Stuttgart, 1927. A model suburb designed by Le Corbusier, Bruno Taut and others, under the direction of Mies van der Rohe.**

Right: **Maxwell Fry's house at New Malden, near Kingston, 1937.**

Private faces in public places
Are wiser and nicer
Than public faces in private places
W. H. AUDEN
Marginalia

It is the natural condition of human beings to make progress by trial and error, and it is the misfortune of our age that the trial and error have been both large-scale and prolonged, with only minimal attention to the question of progress. Planners, architects, developers and housing managers have all been drawn into the same huge plausible vortex – so plausible, indeed, that none of them can be blamed for lacking the foresight to see where it would lead.
ALICE COLEMAN
Utopia on Trial: Vision and Reality in Planned Housing (1985)

But the closest the architects of this period got to Le Corbusier's ideas was Highpoint, a block of flats in Highgate, north London, designed in 1936 by Berthold Lubetkin. With its white rendered façades, ribbon windows, roof garden and overall detachment from its

Highpoint I, designed by Berthold Lubetkin, was praised by Le Corbusier as 'a vertical garden city'.

Kensal House, Maxwell Fry's low-cost housing scheme for the Gas, Light and Coke Company. A nursery school and social facilities were built in an arc of the well of a former gas holder.

surroundings, it was praised by Le Corbusier himself as 'a vertical garden city'. Its success led to the completion of Highpoint II, two years later, next to the original building. They shared a garden, swimming pool, tennis courts and a tea room.

Although Highpoint has become a point of reference for architectural historians, a much more significant development in social housing was taking place in Ladbroke Grove, west London, where Maxwell Fry was commissioned by the Gas, Light and Coke Company to design workers' housing on a former gasworks site. In part it was a publicity stunt to convince people that gas rather than electricity was the fuel of the future. Fry's ideas were based, in both method and form, on those of May in Frankfurt and the Siemensstadt project in Berlin. Many of the tenants of Fry's development, Kensal House, came from the slums of east London. Kitchens and bathrooms were provided, together with separate bedrooms for different members of the family. The flats were arranged in two parallel blocks, each of six storeys, and a nursery school and social facilities were provided in an arc of the well of a former

I have a vision of the Future, chum:
The workers' flats, in fields of soya beans
Towering up like silver pencils, score on
* score,*
While Surging Millions hear the
* Challenge come*
From loudspeakers in communal
* canteens;*
'No Right! No Wrong! All's perfect,
* evermore'.*
JOHN BETJEMAN sending up the
Brave New World of the Welfare State

gas holder. There was a sense of community from the start. The whole operation was carefully managed and tenants encouraged to take part in social events and other communal activities.

An equally significant pre-Second-World-War building was Quarry Hill, an estate of flats in Leeds designed by R. A. H. Livett. It was at that time the largest of its kind, and was to influence much of post-war housing. Livett himself had been influenced by Karl Ehn's Karl-Marx-Hof estate in Vienna. This mammoth apartment block had been dubbed the 'Red Fortress' by the Communist workers who put up a resistance there during civil disturbances in 1934. What brought Quarry Hill into being was a unique combination of government and local politics, together with the technical availability of prefabrication. The design was a combination of the imported French Mopin system of steel frames and reinforced concrete panels, and the Garchey system of ducted waste disposal from each flat. Lifts were provided at every staircase.

Quarry Hill flats in Leeds, modelled on the Karl-Marx-Hof estate in Vienna. The Germans planned to use it as their administrative headquarters for the north of England had an invasion of Britain been successful in the Second World War.

Quarry Hill was an appropriate symbol of the importance of the working class. It was built like a fortress with monumental arched gateways breaching the boundary wall which enclosed the public spaces. Its characteristics were noted during the war by the Germans, who are reputed to have selected it as their future administrative centre for the north of England! Its great urban form became a model for high-density neighbourhoods built in the post-war period, but it was also the precursor of things to come in quite another way: the discovery of corrosion in the steel footings during the 1960s and its use by the local authority for 'decanting' tenants led inevitably to its decline until finally, only 40 years after it was built, Quarry Hill had to be demolished.

During the Second World War about 200,000 houses were destroyed and another 250,000 rendered useless, while only about 200,000 new ones were built. Homes were needed for heroes yet again.

After building licences ended in 1954, there followed a massive

Churchill Gardens, Pimlico, the first major post-war housing scheme, was the result of an architectural competition won by Powell and Moya.

It is quite likely that prefabrication will arrive, on a large scale, before we are practically and aesthetically 'ready', that prefabricated houses will be designed, huckstered, and sold, not for the advantage they can offer, but on the basis of what people are used to, prejudiced in favour of, or, can be titilated by . . .
KARL KOCH
At Home with Tomorrow (1958)

The London County Council's Roehampton Estate, on the edge of Richmond Park, where Le Corbusier's vision took shape in 100 acres of rolling parkland.

programme of building to provide housing, schools, hospitals, universities, power stations, roads and bridges to cater for a population which had grown by 10 million in 20 years.

1946 saw the first significant post-war housing scheme: Churchill Gardens in Pimlico. It had been the result of an architectural competition attracting 65 entries and was won by two young architects, Philip Powell and John Hidalgo Moya. Using Le Corbusier's idea of the *Ville Radieuse,* it comprised 36 blocks of flats built closely together to achieve high density, even though an earlier private scheme at nearby Dolphin Square could boast more people per acre. Long afterwards Pevsner would record: 'The aesthetic significance of Churchill Gardens is that even now, after 25 years, it has remained one of the best estates of its type.'

But the London County Council's architects were to go one better in south-west London, where Le Corbusier's vision took shape on 100 acres of rolling land overlooking Richmond Park, the Alton West Estate,

Roehampton. Here, 1,850 dwellings were provided in 11-storey slab blocks (long and low), 12-storey point blocks (tall and thin), and low-rise maisonettes, with schools, shops, a library and old people's homes to complete the community. The buildings in glass and concrete communicated with their verdant surroundings in a way close to Le Corbusier's model:

> Sun in the house,
> Sky through their windowpanes,
> Trees to look at as soon as they step outside.

Housing was seen as the best way to achieve the socialist vision of the future, or at least a New Jerusalem 'in England's green and pleasant land'. Prefabrication rapidly gained acceptance as the method by which it was to be achieved. The machine would be put to work for the building industry in the same way that it was producing consumer durables, whether refrigerators or motor cars. Mass production would make housing cheap and plentiful; old slums could be cleared away and shortages would be a thing of the past.

It was the start of a process which was to lead eventually to the provision of public housing on an unprecedented scale, and the inevitable split with private-sector housing for sale or rent. Andrew Derbyshire, chairman of Robert Matthew, Johnson-Marshall and Partners, and one of Britain's leading post-war architect–planners, told the Royal Society of Arts in 1985 that his generation believed that Le Corbusier's ideal cities of the 1920s could create order out of the disorder of the Industrial Revolution. 'The master's intoxicating rhetoric and seductive sketches convinced everyone that geometry could rescue people from squalor.' Architects' fixation with form, aided and abetted by prefabrication, led to the often de-humanising use of materials such as concrete, the de-personalisation of the architectural process, and the employment of such technologies as lifts and air conditioning to change people's way of life. The policies of successive governments gave political and economic clout to help the architectural profession realise the dream which Mies van der Rohe had described in 1924: 'I see in industrialisation the central problem of building in our time. If we succeed in carrying out this industrialisation the social, economic, technical and also artistic problems will be readily solved …. It is not so much a question of rationalising existing working methods as of fundamentally re-moulding the whole building trade.'

Governments embarked on the 'numbers game', the race to complete the highest number of dwellings within each administration's period of office as a means of winning electoral support. As Minister of Housing in 1953, Harold Macmillan promised 300,000 new homes a year; by 1964 Harold Wilson had raised the bid to 500,000. Councils were given subsidies to build high: the higher they went, the bigger the subsidy. By 1965 there were 224 industrialised building systems on the

From *Benefactors,* a play by
MICHAEL FRAYN (1984)

They're going to get their houses pulled down whether they like it or not. And we don't need to ask them what they want instead because we know.
— David, an architect, Act One

Skyscrapers, Sheila. That's the answer. That's the only answer. I've tried every other solution, and it doesn't work . . . There'll be endless problems, there'll be endless objections, but I'm going to do it, Sheila. Because in the end it's not art – it's mathematics. A simple equation. You collect up the terms, you get rid of the brackets, you replace all the a's and the b's with the number of three-person households and the length of a coffin and the turning circle of a corporation refuse vehicle – and there at the bottom of the page on the right hand side is the answer: 150 low-rise walk-ups and two socking great skyscrapers.
— David, an architect, Act One

It was people. That's what wrecks all our plans – people.
— David, an architect, Act Two

The strategy of massive slum clearance destroys a valuable social and street life which is impossible to re-establish in new housing forms.

Averaged, standardized accommodation in repetitive blocks precludes the large family, old or single persons and disperses extended families. There is a loss of mutual support and social cohesion, and an increase in loneliness and insecurity.
THEO CROSBY
How to Play the Environment Game
(1973)

Harold Macmillan, as Minister of Housing and Local Government in 1953, promised 300,000 new homes a year.

The association estimates that almost £25-billion is needed to repair all the substandard housing stock in England; another £10-billion is needed to put right design defects, and £15-billion to meet the shortage of housing in Britain. That is a total bill for both private and public sectors of £50-billion – the equivalent of about £1,000 for every man, woman and child in the country.

Evidence given by the
ASSOCIATION OF METROPOLITAN
AUTHORITIES
to the Inquiry on British Housing
(September 1984)

By 1965, there were 224 industrialised building systems available in Britain from 163 developers; 138 of them specifically recommended for housing.
DAVID CRAWFORD
A Decade of British Housing 1963–73
(1975)

Keep your home clean and tidy. Endeavour to have some method of cleaning as you go along; do not try to clean the whole house in one day. Regular bed times for children and adults, except on special occasions. Sit down properly at the table. Hang up your pots and pans or put them on a shelf . . .
Handbook issued by a council
to its tenants in the 1950s,
quoted in
Tenants Take Over
by Colin Ward (1974)

market, 138 of them specifically recommended for housing. Construction workers, many of them only semi-skilled or totally unskilled, were paid on speed rather than on quality of performance.

Only now are we starting to pay the full penalty for the technical (as well as social) failures which date from that period. As Kenneth Campbell, former chief housing architect at the GLC, said: 'We were driven to build numbers and we took it too far. The densities we had to provide and the theories we had to do it seemed to be perfectly good. What we didn't realise was that architects and planners by themselves cannot produce an environment which is satisfactory. Other people have to be involved.'

The principles of the pre-war CIAM (Congrès Internationaux d'Architecture Moderne) were taken up by a new group, Team Ten, whose members included Ralph Erskine – later to embark on the public participation experiment at Byker in Newcastle – and Alison and Peter Smithson, who developed the concept of deck-access blocks with 'streets in the air'; they also had a penchant for exposed concrete and services immortalised in the term 'New Brutalism'.

Between 1957 and 1966 at Park Hill and Hyde Park in Sheffield the Smithsons' theories were to become gruesome reality in a massive estate for 2,000 families on a 50-acre site overlooking the city. The scheme, designed by Lewis Womersley and others, was at first heralded by architects and tenants. But as Martin Pawley recorded in *Architecture versus Housing*:

'The first occupant at Park Hill was a 'trained social worker' who was detailed to provide feedback to the designers on tenant reaction. The intended social relationships based on the existence of 'streets in the air' failed to materialise – only four per cent of the inhabitants 'remembered that (the decks) made it possible to stand and talk to people', while 70 per cent of them complained about the external appearance of the development.'

On the second-stage Hyde Park scheme, the *Architectural Review* allowed itself to criticise the 'regularity' of the inhuman architecture for producing 'an undeniable feeling of living in a barracks'.

Park Hill and Hyde Park, Sheffield, built between 1957 and 1966, were to become home for 2,000 families on a 50-acre site.

Lewis Womersley, City Architect of Sheffield, with his creation, Park Hill Estate in 1962.

No one sweeps a common hall.
CHINESE PROVERB

Slums have their good points; they at least have community spirit and solve the problem of loneliness.
SIR BASIL SPENCE
(1966)

The building of tall blocks without any intrinsic message (they are merely units of accommodation) devalues the identity of the city and robs it of meaningful symbols. In a mass society the identity of the individual is a precious responsibility, to be reinforced at every stage.
THEO CROSBY
How to Play the Environment Game
(1973)

Park Hill was one of the first great post-war schemes to extend Le Corbusier's Unité at Marseilles into a more continuous urban experience, with continuous open access decks every three levels.

Its scale and situation make a monumental contribution to the city but its inhabitants dislike its grim brutality.
THEO CROSBY
How to Play the Environment Game
(1973)

Poor-Law thinking continued to affect the planning of council housing long after the Poor Law itself was dead.
ENID GAULDIE
Cruel Habitations:
A History of Working-Class Housing

Even the best British architects had problems designing housing that suited those who had to live in it. Residents of an estate at Runcorn New Town in Cheshire, designed by James Stirling, one of a handful of British architects with an international reputation, described the outside of the concrete and coloured-glass polyester terraces as inhuman, and likened the houses to 'prison cells'. What the architect had in mind was urban squares which he compared to Queen's Square in Georgian Bath, Bedford Square in Georgian London, and the streets of nearby historic Chester. Yet the terrace houses with their 'washing machine' round windows appear mechanistic, rigid and unresponsive, a finite architectural statement which leaves little room for people to express themselves. The unremitting scale and use of repetitive elements are so often what people criticise most in housing of the period, despite intellectual justifications by the designer of precedent and appropriateness. The Brunswick Centre in Bloomsbury, a development of 560 flats in two facing terraces, with shops and entertainment facilities, Alex-

Above: James Stirling's 'washing machine' housing at Runcorn New Town. Mechanistic, rigid and unresponsive.

Left: Inside one of Stirling's flats, people could express themselves in their usual comforts.

It is astonishing with what savagery planners and architects are trying to obliterate working-class cultural and social patterns. Is it because many of them are first generation middle-class technosnobs?
BRUCE ALLSOPP
Towards a Humane Architecture (1974)

andra Road in St John's Wood, a slightly curving terrace of council flats in pre-cast concrete, and the Thamesmead development, the Greater London Council new town at Erith Marshes, have all been attacked on these grounds, as well as being praised as architectural masterpieces.

Such was the boom in mass housing that by 1965 the GLC could claim to be the largest landlord in the western world. But ten years later 'clean-sweep planning' was itself swept away, as a number of events combined to influence a fresh aproach to housing. In the inner cities of Britain there was rising opposition to wholesale slum clearance programmes from the late 1960s, which in part led to a change of heart by a Labour Government. More importantly, the money had started to run out for public-sector projects. Renewal of existing housing stock became a popular alternative through the provision of home improvement grants and the designation of Housing Action, Housing Priority

Council flats at Alexandra Road, St John's Wood, London. A 'traditional' terrace in pre-cast concrete.

and General Improvement Areas. The role of housing associations was strengthened. Conservation generally was beginning to gain force as a popular movement after the destruction of so many of Britain's historic towns and cities by comprehensive redevelopment schemes.

In 1972, an American, Oscar Newman, published *Defensible Space: People and Design in the Violent City.* In it, he called for relatively modest changes in the way housing estates were designed, which could reduce alienation felt by residents and encourage them to take a responsible attitude to 'invasions of their territory' and the threat of crime. The book received widespread acclaim, and those responsible for mass housing started to look at the estates with fresh eyes. Newman had written that some of the inhabitants of council flats were victimised by society, 'stigmatising them with ugliness, saying with every status symbol available in the architectural language of our culture that living here is falling short of the human state.' The author was concerned that people should personalise their immediate territory, give it identity and look after it – even if that meant introducing a neo-Georgian front door, crazy paving and gnomes in the garden, all anathema to the architectural profession and frowned upon by the local-authority landlords who managed the estates. Bad management, lack of adequate maintenance and the paternalistic attitude of councils presented problems for tenants on most estates. The 'dumping' of problem families together in already badly managed estates only served to exacerbate the situation and hastened the decline and eventual

Thamesmead, the Greater London Council's new town on Erith Marshes, was the setting for Stanley Kubrick's *A Clockwork Orange.*

It is only in a society where we have a government working day and night on our behalf that the housing problems are insoluble.
LORD GOODMAN
Chairman of the Housing Corporation, addressing town planners (1973)

Life is the gift of the immortal gods, living well is the gift of philosophy. Was it philosophy that erected all the towering tenements, so dangerous to the persons who dwell in them? Believe me, that was a happy age, before the days of architects, before the days of builders.
SENECA
(c. 4 BC to AD 65)
in a letter to Lucilius.

Above: The notorious Piggeries in
Liverpool, a social disaster.

Right: Another Liverpool disaster. Oak
and Eldon Gardens, Birkenhead, are
demolished in 1979.

*One of the disastrous things about people
in authority is their capacity for thinking
big. In housing the scale of the problem
has led them to seek gigantic solutions
rather than a multiplicity of solutions,
and rather than help people find their
own solutions . . .*
*Then the people in authority thought big
about flats. A rather sinister combination
of architects, contractors, tower-crane
entrepreneurs, the National Building
Agency and innumerable public relations
consultants littered our cities with tower
blocks, laying up another store of
insoluble problems.*
COLIN WARD
Tenants Take Over (1974)

abandonment of the buildings. Estates across Britain, from Fry's pioneering Kensal House of the 1930s to the notorious 'Piggeries' in Liverpool, became semi-derelict.

Technical failures added to the problems caused by social and management shortcomings. The most dramatic example of this occurred at Ronan Point, a 21-storey tower block in east London. One morning in 1968, the occupant of a flat on the 18th floor of the block lit a match to ignite her gas cooker, which had a faulty connection. The resulting explosion blew out the kitchen wall panel and the ceiling, causing a progressive collapse of the entire corner of the building. Five people died.

The government ordered a public enquiry. It established that the cause of the explosion was a badly fitted nut on the gas supply pipe, but it also came to the controversial conclusion that blame for the subsequent collapse of the building could be not apportioned: fault, if there were any, lay in the regulations which allowed such a structure to be built.

Simon Jenkins, in *Landlords to London,* wrote of the affair:

'Many residents of high-rise flats had long assumed that their discontent with this form of living was a private problem which they would have to sort out themselves. They assumed, because that is what they had been told, that high living was part of the price of progress in the modern world. The terraced housing which had for centuries knitted together London's communities, it was said, no longer yielded acceptable standards of open space, nor was it architecturally exciting enough. The collapse of Ronan Point unleashed the fear and frustration which people subjected to these arguments had long felt and led to a deep revulsion against a form of housing which over a decade had been almost a craze among local authority and government architects. It was a form characterised not by the textbook pictures of gleaming towers, blue skies and green lawns, but by broken lifts, vandalised passages, filthy entrances, windy, unkempt open spaces and the absence of any sense of homeliness. Relations between housing managers and tenants often became ones of mutual recrimination if not open warfare. And the pride which should have come from community ownership was seldom in evidence.'

In the wake of the collapse of Ronan Point, more than £100 million was spent in Britain on strengthening – or rather, holding together – 567 tower blocks containing 38,700 flats of similar construction. At least 10,000 dwellings built since 1970 were torn down within 15 years of their construction due to fundamental defects.

Britain was not the only country to suffer such disasters.

In 1955 a vast project had opened in St Louis, Missouri, called Pruitt-Igoe. It was designed by Minoru Yamasaki, architect of the World Trade Center in New York, and the American Institute of Architects gave it an award. Here too were 'streets of air', but they were not enough to encourage the sort of middle-class lifestyle expected of the residents.

The jacket of J. G. Ballard's science fiction novel, *High-Rise,* about the collapse of society when technology breaks down.

Modern architecture died in St Louis, Missouri, on July 15, 1972 at 3.32 pm (or thereabouts) when the infamous Pruitt-Igoe scheme, or rather several of its slab blocks, were given the final coup de grâce by dynamite. Previously it had been vandalised, mutilated and defaced by its black inhabitants, and although millions of dollars were pumped back, trying to keep it alive (fixing the broken elevators, repairing smashed windows, repainting), it was finally put out of its misery. Boom, boom, boom.
CHARLES JENCKS
The Language of Post-Modern Architecture (Fourth Edition 1984)

In fact it died in Britain four years earlier in Canning Town, east London, on 16 May 1968 at 5.45 am (or thereabouts). A gas explosion caused the partial collapse of Ronan Point, a 21-storey residential tower block. Five people were killed and 17 injured. CK.

Ronan Point, the east London tower block, the morning a gas explosion on the eighteenth floor caused the collapse of the south-east corner of the building, killing five people.

The best thing that ever happened to British architecture was the collapse of Ronan Point.
THEO CROSBY
How to Play the Environment Game
(1973)

The projects are hideous, of course, there being a law, apparently respected throughout the world, that popular housing shall be as cheerless as a prison.
JAMES BALDWIN
Nobody Knows My Name

It is not generally appreciated that the prime determinants of the built environment are not in any sense architectural. Economic, political, commercial and social factors control most of the major design decisions to such an extent that the actual designer has, all too often, to devote his ingenuity to making the best of a bad job, finding a way to bend the rules to create something which is remotely humane. An obvious example of this is the Housing Cost Yardstick, a bureaucratic cost control tool which has been inflated into the principal determinant in public sector housing. The whole economic and fiscal context in which he works forces the architect to cut initial capital costs at the expense of future cost in use.
Evidence given by the
ROYAL INSTITUTE OF BRITISH ARCHITECTS
to the UN conference on the Human
Environment (June 1972)

Social problems crept in; people moved out, and the estate declined.

In 1971 a meeting was held of all those left in the building and at last someone got round to asking them what they wanted. Their reply was unequivocal. 'Blow it . . . *up!* Blow it . . . *up!*' they chanted. On 15 July 1972, the three central blocks were reduced to rubble.

As dynamite brought down Pruitt-Igoe, Paul Rudolph, dean of the Yale School of Architecture, was putting up the Oriental Gardens project in New Haven. It was meant to be a model of urban renewal, but its prefabricated modules did not fit together too well. By September

1980 there were only 17 tenants left in the leaky, draughty flats. Early the following year, the federal government's Department of Housing and Urban Development, which had commissioned the building, decided to demolish it.

The legacy of the high-rise housing disaster is still with us. Tenants' groups have organised themselves on a national basis to investigate problem estates and to lobby for rehousing. Councils, meanwhile, will be paying off the loans for these blocks until about 2030.

In the early 1970s, vast medium- and low-rise blocks were still being built. Aylesbury Estate in Southwark, south London, claimed to be 'the largest system-built housing block in Europe'. But new estates like Lillington Gardens in Pimlico, south-west London, by architects Darbourne and Darke, were beginning to appear. While being of very high density (nearly 200 people per acre, more than many high-rise schemes) they also gave the impression of being up-market, individually designed flats. Some speculative house builders started using Neo-Vernacular or Neo-Georgian styles. New life was given to thousands of Victorian terrace homes with the aid of government and local authority improvement grants.

So what went wrong in the design and management of high-rise buildings? Research by Dr Alice Coleman into more than 4,000 blocks

The demolition of Pruitt-Igoe.

The government is America's biggest slum landlord. More than 2.4 million people live in over 800,000 public housing units, characterised by inoperable plumbing, heating, doors and windows and arbitrarily regulated by a generally hostile management. These notoriously deplorable conditions begin from lack of tenant control and poor project design, constructed with too little money and too much graft. 'New' units are slums in ten years, often as few as five. Drugs, vandalism and crime follow this deterioration, public housing tenants have been understandably plagued by fear, apathy and hopelessness. But they stay – there's no place else to go.
From *Catalog No. 2: Communities/ Housing*
The Swallow Press, Chicago (1972)

Lillington Gardens.

On the one hand we have supralocal agencies which plan for and provide for people's housing needs, with the result that the people so planned for and provided for turn into consumers or passive beneficiaries. On the other hand, if housing is treated as verbal entity, as a means to human ends, as an activity rather than as a manufactured and packaged product, decision-making power must, of necessity, remain in the hands of the users themselves. I will go beyond that to suggest that the ideal we should strive for is a model which conceives housing as an activity in which the users – as a matter of economic, social and psychological common sense – are the principal actors.

JOHN TURNER
'Housing as a Verb' in
Freedom to Build: Dweller Control of the Housing Process (1972).

Our vast housing problems machine has committed one blunder after another in the name of social betterment. The betterment is often hard to find, especially if compared with what might have been, but the malaise and misery and tragedy are writ large as soon as one opens one's eyes to the facts. The brave new Utopia is essentially a device for treating people like children, first by denying them the right to choose their own kind of housing, and then by choosing for them disastrous designs that create a needless sense of social failure . . . Housing choice and responsibility for one's home should be decisions made not by the bureaucrats but by the occupants. The future should be in their own hands.

ALICE COLEMAN
Utopia on Trial: Vision and Reality in Planned Housing (1985)

across Britain, carried out over a five-year period and completed in 1985, reveals that various features of large estates contributed to their failure: neglected common space, long alleyways and escape routes for vandals and criminals, and the oppressive scale and unnecessary height of the buildings. She concludes that no more tower blocks should be built and makes recommendations on how existing estates could be improved. While her ideas are largely confirmation of Newman's on 'defensible space', they are the result of the first objective analysis in Britain, and effectively expressed in her book *Utopia on Trial*: 'The brave new Utopia is essentially a device for treating people like children, first by denying them the right to choose their own kind of housing, and then by choosing for them disastrous designs that create a needless sense of social failure.' She believes the suburban semi-detached is the most successful example of housing yet devised and advocates return-ing all housing initiatives to the free market 'so that architects, builders and developers can become responsive to residents' needs'.

But examples of a more democratic approach to public sector archi-tecture are emerging. One of the most successful schemes is the Byker development in Newcastle-upon-Tyne by Ralph Erskine, Vernon Gracie and Roger Tillotson. Commissioned in 1968, the architects decided to change the approach to mass housing by making it more

Reality of fiction
Sir, I read in the Press that the set for the BBC's new soap opera East Enders *has been designed to last for 15 years. How many of the tower, deck entry and other blocks of modern flats built in the real life East End in recent years can be said to have the same life span, at least in the sense of providing satisfaction to their inhabitants?*

We may truly be said to live in a television age when what we see on the screen has more durability than the reality it portrays.
Yours faithfully,
CHRISTOPHER TUGENDHAT
Letter to the Editor in
The Times (18 February 1985)

Ownership, or a long lease, ensures an involvement in the quality and maintenance of a dwelling. At present publicly owned housing is administered in a way that excludes personal responsibility or social control.

Large buildings offer maximum scope for vandalism, because responsibility and control are remote. Children are difficult to control or protect from above four storeys.

The necessity for economy in construction ensures that most tower blocks are underserviced. Lifts are particularly vulnerable.

Personal identity comes largely from possessions and we must create in all housing the possibility of ownership and community involvement.

Without ownership the dwelling is not maintained or improved.

Without communal responsibility, gardens, fountains and sculpture are vandalised out of protest or boredom.
THEO CROSBY
How to Play the Environment Game
(1973)

It would be foolish to suggest that the tenant take-over is not a political matter. It is political in the most profound sense: it is about the distribution of power in society. But fortunately it is one of those issues which cuts across normal party divisions. It finds supporters amongst adherents of all political parties, and none. Its advocates ought to exploit this spectrum of support.

COLIN WARD
Tenants Take Over (1974)

Opposite: Ralph Erskine and a resident of Byker in the architect's office, a disused funeral parlour on the site (see p. 200).

Right and *below*: The Brinkburn Street area and Albion Road, Byker, in the mid 1960s.

human and seeking direct participation by the residents. New homes and flats were provided here for 10,000 people on the 200-acre site, with the preservation of the social unity of the existing community being the primary intention. The job architect and several of his colleagues lived on site, working from an office in a disused funeral parlour! The architects' office became something of a social centre.

Ralph Erskine wrote:

'People, kids, the chief planner – they all come in and out. We often took in kids who had been "chucked out" from home and it was raining … And you could walk out on site and talk to people and contractors. We exhibited plans, drawings and models in the window – but also local notices. "Anyone lost a tricycle? Ask the architect." "Guinea pigs … " and so on. Much less important was the RIBA sign-plate.'

A huge 'wall' of housing was built first, to screen the rest of the site from traffic noise and cold northerly winds. Built in a sinuous ribbon which varies between 5 and 8 storeys, more than half a mile long, its form was however broken down into identifiable sections, with patterned brickwork in shades of red, brown and yellow, and by timber balconies to the south. Byker is a low-rise estate, and much attention has been given to circulation space, roads, playgrounds, shopping and social facilities. Shops and offices have been inserted into small housing blocks, providing a normal urban mix. Variety and surprise, planting, and creative use of what would otherwise be left-over space, have all been achieved within normal housing cost-yardsticks. Despite the inventive and unconventional design of the new building, familiar landmarks such as churches and pubs were retained and incorporated into the community. Byker even won an award for the 'Best Kept Village in Britain', a unique achievement for a mass-housing scheme.

Jane Jacobs, who has studied urban problems in America for several decades, believes that the solution to inner-city ills does not rest entirely with architects and planners, but in understanding how cities work and tapping other people's skills, particularly through public involvement. That process started in Britain nearly twenty years ago and looks certain to blossom. The next problem is to find adequate resources to repair and replace a largely Victorian housing stock; one of Britain's less impressive statistics is that we spend less on housing today than any other Western country. At the present level of activity, it has been predicted, 'the housing problem' will be with us for another 900 years.

For those in the private sector, speculative builders have been able to supply hundreds of thousands of new homes each year: mostly two-storey terraced, semi-detached or detached houses, with gardens and often a garage, and in traditional materials such as brick, with pitched, tiled roofs. Owner–occupiers do not share most of the problems associated with large-scale, publicly owned blocks: they have control over decisions on repair and maintenance, privacy, and when to sell up and move on.

The need to give one's personal stamp is as important as the inclination to be unobtrusive. In short, it has to do with the need for a personal environment where one can do as one likes; indeed it concerns one of the strongest urges of mankind: the desire for possession.

Now possession is different from property. We may possess something which is not our property, and conversely something may be our property which we do not possess. Property is a legal term, but the idea of possession is deeply rooted in us. In the light of our subject, it is therefore important to realise that possession is inextricably linked with action. To possess something we have to take possession. We have to make it part of ourselves, and it is therefore necessary to reach out for it. To possess something we have take it in our hand, touch it, test it, put our stamp on it. Something becomes our possession because we make a sign on it, because we give it our name, or defile it, because it shows traces of our existence.

N. J. HABRAKEN
Supports: an Alternative to Mass Housing (1972)

When dwellers control the major decisions and are free to make their own contribution to the design, construction or management of their housing, both the process and the environment produced stimulate individual and social well-being. When people have no control over, nor responsibility for key decisions in the housing process, on the other hand, dwelling environments may instead become a barrier to personal fulfilment and a burden on the economy.

JOHN TURNER and
ROBERT FICHTER
Freedom to Build (1972)

Prevention [of further social housing failures] would seem to lie in a decision to build no more flats and concentrate on houses instead, but the question arises as to what sort of houses. The various test measures show that inter-war houses consistently perform better than those of either the pre-1914 or post-1945 vintage. Modern house designs seems to have deteriorated over the decades as the DOE has recommended increasingly undesirable designs, for example, faceless facades and the abandonment of the traditional streetscape.

ALICE COLEMAN
Utopia on Trial: Vision and Reality in Planned Housing (1985)

Design modification would need to bring about only a 10 per cent drop in levels of litter, graffiti, vandalism, excrement and the number of children in care to achieve more than all the Utopian efforts of government over the last 40 years. In practice, however, we expect it to achieve far more, including a spin-off in the reduction of stress and trauma, mental illness and crime.

ALICE COLEMAN
Utopia on Trial: Vision and Reality in Planned Housing (1985)

To the private house-builder, the main problem is land supply in relation to demand. Pressure is highest in those regions where employment and the economy generally are most active, leading to a sharp division between house prices in the north and the south-east. Building land fetches ever-higher prices: £200,000 per acre was not uncommon in 1985, or even £380,000 in Berkshire, the prime residential county near London, for example. In 1960, land used to account for 10 per cent of the total price of a house; in 1985 it was nearer 40 per cent. The Green Belt surrounding Britain's towns and cities faces an onslaught as companies like Consortium Developments, a group of the country's largest house-builders, try to persuade local authorities and the Government to release land for mini new towns.

While the modern owner-occupied house is vastly superior in some respects to its predecessors, such as thermal insulation, the cost of land has meant smaller gardens; the cost of good-quality timber has led to almost universal use of cheaper softwoods for roof trusses spaced closely together (preventing the use of the loft for storage and extension) and for doors and windows which cannot be expected to last for more than a few years, and the high cost of borrowing money from banks and building societies has led to a reduction in space standards. More emphasis is being placed on electrical 'white' goods such as kitchen accessories, and on interior décor, a North American pattern. House builders are even talking about the house as just another 'consumer durable', an attitude which would convert the house into a depreciating liability rather than the appreciating asset which owner–occupiers have come to expect as a matter of course in Britain.

A typical owner-occupied home of the 1980s, built by Barratt Developments.

A FUTURE
FOR THE PAST

Time present and time past
Are both perhaps present in time future
And time future contained in time past.
T. S. ELIOT
Burnt Norton

Conservation is a comparatively new idea.

MICHAEL MANSER
President of the RIBA (1983-5)
writing in
The Financial Times (11 January 1984)

If any person for the sake of traffic [i.e. profit] should have purchased any building, in hopes of gaining more by pulling it down than the sum for which he bought it, he shall be obliged to pay into the exchequer double the sum for which he purchased it.

ROMAN INSCRIPTION
prior to AD 63, condemning demolition as 'the most cruel kind of traffic in Herculaneum.'

Both are quoted in *Our Vanishing Heritage* by Marcus Binney (1984)

For anything to be real it must be local.
G. K. CHESTERTON

The concert hall at Snape, an 850-seat auditorium built within an East Anglian malt house, by Arup Associates.

The British revere the past, and for the most part resist change. It is partly for these reasons that they like to retain old buildings rather than see their 'heritage' diminished by demolition.

The conservation movement thrives on nostalgia, on a sense of history, and on psychological dependence on the familiar. But it is also considerably strengthened by a widespread sense of loss caused by the comprehensive post-war redevelopment which has left few towns and cities untouched. There is often dissatisfaction at the modern architecture which now stands on the sites of much-loved buildings that have been demolished. It is hardly surprising that the British, for all or any of these reasons, prefer to cling to the apron strings of the past rather than accept the stark and frequently inhuman buildings of the present.

The conservation movement gathered momentum from the mid 1950s, when new construction was changing the face of the country, bringing with it a growing scepticism about whether the new was necessarily better than what it replaced. Conservation societies began to spring up; most of those in existence today were founded since the late 1950s. Conservation in Britain can be seen as a long-running campaign to save old buildings, punctuated every few years by a major battle which turns the matter into a public issue, often bitterly contested. Much modern architecture has been of an alien scale, quality and character, and does not respond to the 'spirit of the place', the context, in which it is built, thus reinforcing prejudice against the new.

The first major conservation battle after the Second World War concerned not an entire building, but an arch. Designed by Philip Hardwick, it had stood at the entrance of Euston Station for well over a hundred years. The Euston Arch only came to be seen as valuable when its life was threatened – supposedly to accommodate longer platforms which in the event were not extended – but the fight over its future was a mere skirmish compared to the full-scale battles that were to come.

It is easier to build two chimneys than to maintain one.
ENGLISH PROVERB

It is . . . no question of expediency or feeling whether we shall preserve the buildings of past times or not. We have no right whatever to touch them. They are not ours. They belong partly to those who built them, and partly to all the generations of mankind who are to follow us. The dead have still their right in them.
JOHN RUSKIN
Seven Lamps of Architecture (1849)

We should make the old serve the new.
MAO TSE-TUNG

The capacity of historical architecture to employ our perception and imagination for a long time establishes a psychological connexion between us and our environment, the latter being experienced as 'interesting'. In comparison, average modern architecture offers remarkably little visual information. Neither does the modern repertoire contain any symbolic aspect nor any considerable amount of 'aesthetic information'. Working to a general grid pattern the new architecture explores the principal of endless addition and repetition of a few elemental norms: once we have seen the corner we have seen the whole. Normally the effect is monotony and our reaction boredom, if significance is not achieved by unusual height or outline.
THEO CROSBY
How to Play the Environment Game (1973)

Demonstrators trying to save the Euston Arch (*inset*) in 1961. Their protests over its demolition were in vain.

British Railways, wishing to push forward with a modernisation programme, applied to demolish the Arch. After numerous inquiries and determined efforts to save it, the Prime Minister, Harold Macmillan, approved its demolition in 1962. Although the campaign to save the Arch was lost, the affair stiffened the resolve of the conservation lobby never again to allow redevelopment plans to replace a valued or well-loved building or area. It was a brave and somewhat unworldly position to adopt, for ranged against them were some formidable opponents. At the time, the Euston Arch campaigners were seen as sentimental fuddy-duddies determined to hold back the thrusting men of property who wanted not to grace London with elegant architecture, but to put up buildings that would yield a high return. For the most part, the men of property commanded the stage in the 1950s and '60s. This was the period of comprehensive redevelopment in many cities. It was the property deals and the dismal architecture which arose out of them that further reduced the standing of architects and architecture. It also convinced the conservationists that right, if not might, was on their side.

Although major redevelopment of London had taken place between the wars, the scale and pace of new projects took off after the lifting of building licences in 1954. Land prices jumped and dozens of schemes were prepared. The late 1950s saw more and more plans for taller and larger office blocks: New Zealand House at the bottom of Haymarket, and Castrol and Bowater House are just three examples. In 1959 the number of deals in property shares jumped from 16,000 to 102,000, and Jack Cotton's controversial plan for Piccadilly Circus was published. The trend continued. 1962 saw the rise of blocks such as the Shell Centre on the South Bank (351 ft), the Vickers Tower at Millbank (387 ft), and the Hilton Hotel on Park Lane (328 ft). In 1964 the Barbican scheme took shape in the form of tower blocks on London Wall. Bulldozers moved on to 13 acres of Georgian and Victorian terraces along Euston Road to make way for the Euston Centre. In 1965, Centre Point, symbol of the post-war property boom, was completed. The building remained empty for fifteen years, but continued to increase in value while not earning a penny in rent.

By the mid 1960s, more than a hundred property millionaires had been created. The most famous of these was Harry Hyams, developer of Centre Point, who reputedly amassed a fortune of £27 million by the age of 39. But the cost in environmental terms was also dear. In an age of protest people began to fight back.

During 1972 Christopher Booker, who as early as 1962 had written a ferocious attack on tower blocks of flats in *Private Eye*, the satirical magazine which he then edited, wrote a series of articles with Benny Grey for the *Eye*, *The Sunday Times* and *The Observer*, winning them the Campaigning Journalists of the Year award. As the property developers worked by stealth, publicity was unwelcome to them. But it also alerted people and moulded the public's response. The 'Nooks and

Nooks and Corners

of the New Barbarism:1. Hillgate House, Ludgate Hill

"... a large modern group by Theo Birks ... It looks promising at the time of writing" - Professor Doctor Nikolaus Pevsner. *Buildings of Britain (City and Westminster, 1962).*

No. We did not get Reynolds Stone to design the lettering over the front door in Old Bailey. The Board of Trade which took over the building when we couldn't let it to anyone else chose this. To compensate we have emphasized to the outside public the essentially upward line of the staircase to the first floor. A plank of wood in the form of an ungrippable bannister rail continues the upward line and is itself a forward-looking feature of its time.

To show that this is a modern building we have deliberately off-centred the prominent features on an otherwise restrained facade. This has been skillfully done by the introduction of a concrete projection which, though affording no shelter, performs the function of drawing the eye down to the door and window which are themselves off centre with the projection. The effect of weather further emphasises the downward line and contrasts with the plain serenity of the facade in a happy way. We had not, of course, calculated on the demands of the London Fire Service, but I think the fire hydrant notice and the triple fire alarms are rather fun. To add to them is the exciting intrusion of the street name "Old Bailey" kindly awarded by the Corporation of the City of London. To bind the whole composition together and to suggest a vertical motif the strips either side of this facade are of purple mosaic.

John Betjeman

The action of time makes man's works into natural objects . . . In making them natural objects also time gives to man's life-less productions the brief quality of everything belonging to nature – life.

VERNON LEE

In Praise of Old Houses (1902)

We must beware of contempt for old buildings just because, like old people, they can be frail, muddled and squalid. That contempt can easily become a sort of architectural fascism. Not all our slums are slums. Piecemeal renewal, each piece in scale with the place, is not necessarily a wrong answer just because it is an old one.

LIONEL BRETT, VISCOUNT ESHER

'Preservation after Buchanan' (1964)

People spend so much of their time on holiday and at weekends going to see buildings of the past because they are a pleasure. You don't get people going to look at modern buildings as part of a pleasure concern; they go to look at old buildings because they are fun. They don't go and look at the square slab blocks of the 1930s, but they do go to the Chrysler Building, the Empire State Building and the Rockefeller Center which are decorative modern buildings.

TERRY FARRELL

(1985)

Sir John Betjeman's first *Private Eye* column in 1971.

Corners' (of the 'New Barbarism') column first appeared as a regular *Private Eye* feature in 1971, written by Sir John Betjeman (even though those who read his 'gentle but deadly' articles did not at first believe that he had penned them). He was succeeded by his daughter, Candida (latterly Lycett Green) and then Gavin Stamp, under the pen-name of 'Piloti'. Booker was also responsible for one of the first alternative development schemes, when he tried to save the nineteenth-century Tolmers Square buildings at Euston from a huge office proposal.

By the mid 1970s, the pendulum had swung against wholesale redevelopment, and there was a collapse of architectural self-confidence which continued into the '80s. 'For the first time we had seen the future, and it did not work,' wrote Christopher Booker. 'Our architectural and cultural self-confidence disintegrated with quite astounding speed.' Anonymous architecture, largely the product of the anonymous patronage of banks, insurance and pension funds, was now out of court in the public's esteem.

By 1977, when the bulldozer and ball and chain had been to some extent brought under control, it was possible for Booker to assess the real damage. 'Firstly, far from believing that anything new is better, we are now (generally) convinced of almost exactly the reverse – that anything new is worse, and that almost any old building should be preserved at all costs. So total is our lack of confidence in our ability to design, to plan, even to build properly, that we are now prepared to revere almost any building from "the past" – not just masterpieces, or Georgian terraces, but grim Victorian warehouses, factories, back-to-back jerry-built Victorian slums, even the serried ranks of suburban semis of the 1920s and 1930s.

'But secondly, and here is the rub, as our society continues to change with great speed, old buildings still continue to outlive their original uses. Churches, railway stations, warehouses, town halls, country houses continue to become redundant, or "uneconomical" in ever-greater numbers. But just as we can no longer bear to think of anything old being pulled down, so we desperately switch all our architectural skills, our resources and our cultural ingenuity to adapting these old structures to new uses. Churches become concert halls, warehouses become "World Trade Centres", country houses become museums (or "garden centres" or "equestrian centres"). Cotswold tithe barns become trendy restaurants.'

Attempts to preserve or recreate the past have progressed much further since then. Even the façades of relatively undistinguished Victorian commercial buildings are retained as death-masks to new buildings behind, a requirement of planning committees too frightened of the architect's alternative elevations; and dormer windows have become almost a prerequisite for planning permission in some inner London boroughs. This apparent preoccupation with the past prompted Michael Manser, President of the Royal Institute of British Architects 1983–5, to champion the cause of freedom of expression for architects and to take up the battle cry that 'conservation has gone too far.'

William Morris was instrumental in establishing conservation as a subject of public concern in Britain. In 1877 he founded the Society for the Protection of Ancient Buildings, following a furious debate over what type and degree of restoration was appropriate for various historic buildings. This led in 1882 to the first Ancient Monuments Act to preserve earthworks and unoccupied ruins; similar legislation had been in force in France for nearly forty years. The idea of including houses of historical interest in this legislation was later condemned by Lord Curzon as 'an outrageous attack on private property'. But it was the war years of 1939–45 which really alerted people to the need to care for the past, as bombing destroyed much of historic cities such as Bath.

In 1968 four major conservation studies were launched in Bath, Chester, Chichester and York, and the next year the first British national survey of buildings was completed, with a list of 120,000 properties. It soon became clear that many 'marginal' buildings were lost as owners, intent on selling or redeveloping, attempted to avoid listing. The hasty destruction of the Art Deco Firestone factory in London in 1980, just days before it was due to be listed, so appalled the conservation-minded Environment Secretary, Michael Heseltine, that

The destruction of the Firestone Factory, west London, one Bank Holiday weekend in 1980, led to an accelerated re-survey of the country's listed buildings.

With the passing of each [historic building] goes a slice of social history – a thread of civilisation. Surely we can learn to reweave those threads in a bright new context, so that our children and grandchildren can respond, as we have, to the challenge of beauty created hundreds of years ago?
THE COUNTESS OF DARTMOUTH
Do You Care about Historic Buildings?
(1970)

Conservation is bound to involve preservation, but it is more than preservation: it is bringing an area back to life.
COLIN BUCHANAN & PARTNERS
Bath: a Study in Conservation (1968)

The conservation movement is an expression of the concern that material progress should not be self-defeating.
Evidence given by
THE BURTON ST LEONARDS SOCIETY, Sussex
to the UN conference on the Human Environment (June 1972)

Planning is the means of conservation; it is also the means of total destruction.
Evidence given by
PERSHORE CIVIC SOCIETY, Worcestershire
to the UN conference on the Human Environment (June 1972)

The Circus, Bath. The city's identity has been preserved through a strictly enforced policy on conservation.

he ordered an accelerated re-survey, which for the first time included buildings of the inter-war years.

The re-survey, involving 92 listers, was begun in 1982 by what is now the Historic Buildings and Monuments Commission (popularly known as English Heritage), for completion in 1987. By then, some 500,000 buildings and structures will be listed in a new Domesday Book of British heritage, including eighteenth-century milestones, early pillar-boxes, chest tombs and even cast-iron urinals, as well as the finest country houses in the land. Only the grade – I, II* or II – will reflect their relative importance. The most heavily listed places in Britain are Berwick-on-Tweed and Bath, and the re-survey has revealed nearly a thousand medieval buildings in addition to those already listed. The biggest increase is in dwellings, with a three- or four-fold increase; some towns and villages have seen the number of protected structures increase from, for example, 7 to 100, as at Warmington in Oxfordshire. The current lists end in 1939, although there is a draft shortlist of 50 post-war buildings. In Scotland a 30-year rule applies, meaning that buildings completed in 1955 are eligible for listing in 1985, a requirement which many would like to see introduced in England.

While official listing policy has saved many old buildings, and the National Trust (now with more than a million members) acts as guardian to many of the finest properties in the land, much recent conservation work has relied on voluntary effort. One of the most active pressure groups is SAVE Britain's Heritage, founded in 1975. SAVE has been a well-organised thorn in the side of developers and demolishers and can be credited with helping to save a number of buildings, but possibly more importantly, it has raised and sustained public awareness of conservation issues. Over the past decade, SAVE has mounted a series of exhibitions at the Victoria and Albert Museum on conservation themes, including the decay of country houses and the future of redundant churches.

In addition to its primary aim of conserving existing buildings, SAVE

If conservationists were honest men – instead of politicians and impresarios in disguise – they would preserve their ancient structures like New Guinean cargo-cult airports – waiting for the second coming of the vanished social and economic structure that made them once make sense.
MARTIN PAWLEY
'A question for the conservationists' in *RIBA Journal* (December 1984)

The site of the proposed Mansion House scheme.

The need now is to establish coexistence between past and present creations. As Randolph Langenbach asked in A Future from the Past, *'Is it not better to add to the sum total of the record of human creativity than to subtract from it?' Are there not enough opportunities for new buildings without destroying fine or worthwhile buildings from the past?*

MARCUS BINNEY

'Oppression to obsession' in
Our Past Before Us
edited by David Lowenthal and Marcus Binney (1981)

Mies van der Rohe's office block superimposed on a photograph of the Mansion House Square site. The Prince of Wales called it a 'giant glass stump better suited to downtown Chicago'.

also proposes new uses for old buildings. Re-using old buildings for quite different purposes is a relatively new approach to conservation, but one that is gaining increasing support from architects, particularly those who accept that this is a legitimate part of contemporary architecture.

Apart from trying to find economic new uses for old buildings, SAVE's work has increasingly been to propose alternative redevelopment plans; conservation has gone on the offensive. Of particular note are the schemes prepared for Billingsgate Market and Broad Street station, in the City of London (now demolished); the conversion of Battersea power station – the 'Colossus of Battersea' – into a themed leisure centre; and Terry Farrell's plan to save most of the Victorian commercial buildings on the proposed Mansion House Square site, in the City of London, as an alternative to their demolition to make way for a Mies van der Rohe office block.

The 27-year ambition of property developer Peter Palumbo to build Mies's design became the most celebrated of all post-Second-World-War planning battles over a work of architecture. At a public inquiry in 1984, the scheme was supported by most of the architectural establishment, but opposed by the City Corporation, the Greater London

Council, the Royal Fine Art Commission, the Victorian Society and SAVE. The Palumbo supporters argued that 'excellence' should be the deciding factor; that London did not have one world-class building of the latter half of the twentieth century; and that the listed buildings on the site were second-rate. Above all they argued that the City needed modern buildings if it was to remain one of the world's financial centres.

The inquiry inspector, and eventually the Secretary of State for the Environment, Patrick Jenkin, decided this particular scheme was wholly inappropriate, in scale and height, and that the medieval street pattern should be preserved. It was only a partial victory for the conservationists, however, as the way was left clear for Palumbo to commission a new architect to design a fresh scheme which could also do away with the existing buildings. Within a few weeks of the inquiry decision, James Stirling was appointed to prepare new plans.

Architect Terry Farrell, who practises in London, believes that existing buildings should be treasured for their own qualities, and that they can usually be adapted to new uses. Indeed, they often lend themselves to the most technologically advanced industries such as television. He converted a large garage at Camden Town, north London, into TV-am's studios, adding decorative features and colour to brighten up the working environment. Offices and production areas for 400 people were provided in areas once used to repair and service cars. Similarly, a group of former banana and rum warehouses in London's Docklands were partly gutted and rebuilt as studios for Limehouse Productions.

Historic buildings, like businesses, often demand an entrepreneurial approach. Those who see them principally as a burden are of two types. One is the speculator, the developer who wishes to be rid of them for financial gain. The other is the administrator, who grudges the time and money absorbed in looking after older buildings or lacks the expertise, advice or imagination to see how they could be adapted in a practical and economic way. Both types are often obsessed by the idea that a new building replacing the old one will somehow be magically maintenance-free.
MARCUS BINNEY
'Oppression to obsession' in
Our Past Before Us (1981)

Terry Farrell's alternative plan for Mansion House Square. He aimed to adapt most of the existing buildings.

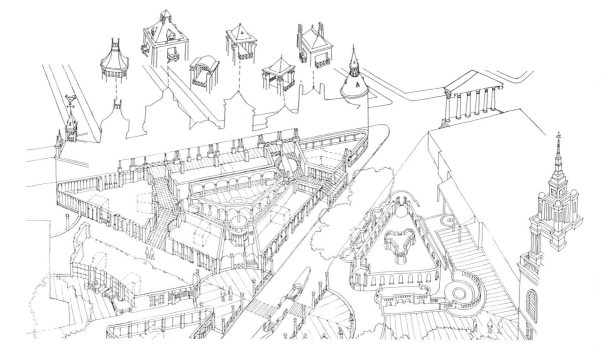

There is something about a building which is akin to the quality we refer to in humans as 'personality'. We even use the same words of them – buildings are noble, mysterious, friendly or forbidding. No great architecture can exist without emotion. When architecture is reduced to a mere intellectual exercise, it is sterile.
RALPH TUBBS
The Englishman Builds (1945)

The skilful adaption of the Maltings at Snape as a concert hall, with new roof trusses, a restaurant and lobbies.

'Much of the success [of grafting new buildings on to old] depends on knowing what not to do, what to leave undone,' wrote professor of architecture Michael Brawne about the work of Arup Associates. Arup have carried out many sensitive alterations to existing structures, such as the redevelopment of Truman's Brewery in Brick Lane, east London, the RNAS building at the naval base in Portsmouth, and the rebuilding of the Maltings concert hall at Snape in Suffolk following a serious fire in 1969. The Maltings were described by architect and Cambridge lecturer David Roberts as 'the best example of modern British architecture.' The buildings appear from outside to be virtually untouched; inside there are new roof trusses, stairs, lobbies and a restaurant, all of which blend naturally with the existing structure.

To the casual passer-by, beautifully crafted old buildings provide landmarks and points of reference, especially in the urban landscape. Some would argue, like Sir Hugh Casson, that to build almost always means to destroy. Yet there are, it seems, unlimited opportunities to

preserve the best and let the worst go in any redevelopment plans. While many might agree that conservation has gone too far, only about 1 per cent of all buildings in London for example, are listed, leaving a potential 99 per cent for demolition; certain areas are more protected than others – for example, 60 per cent of Westminster and 30 per cent of the City of London are now legally protected conservation areas. The idiosyncratic and unique – such as Michelin House in Fulham Road, Chelsea, a good example of architecture as corporate advertising, festooned with references to the early history of motoring and bulging with tyre motifs – are particularly worth saving and converting to new uses once their intended life (original use span) has come to an end. In this case the building is being restored and converted into offices, a retail store and restaurant.

In Britain the conservation movement can be seen in the much wider context of urban renewal, with the switch in recent years from building new to refurbishing the old. The era of the post-war New Towns has ended and efforts are now being directed towards reviving what are largely medieval Georgian and Victorian towns and cities. It is a process of consolidation re-using the existing infrastructure rather than abandoning it to build on green-field sites. One of the main concerns is to try to preserve the individual identity of a place – so that Bath does not

Michelin House, an example of architecture as corporate advertising, which found a new lease of life as a retail store, restaurant and offices.

Fear of contagion with alien ideas is the main deterrent to curiosity. Although in bygone days an architect's education was incomplete without a first hand acquaintance with old cultures, the present generation is loath to learn travel's lessons. 'Travel,' says Harry Weese, a prominent architect, 'is a two-edged thing. It can go to an architect's head, leading to cultural disorientation.'
BERNARD RUDOFSKY
Streets for People:
A Primer for Americans (1969)

Some of a city's diversity, historic continuity and character is destroyed when old buildings are razed. The historic significance of architectural styles is as indisputable as the historic events surrounding them. After all, we do not throw out the wedding pictures of our parents because their dress now looks funny, or because the pictures are not quite so wonderful as we once thought they were.
WOLF VON ECKARDT
in *Time* magazine

The Ghirardelli chocolate factory in San Francisco was converted into a leisure shopping area of shops, cafés, restaurants and a theatre.

become like Newcastle-upon-Tyne, nor London like New York or Chicago – and to use a new and varied mixture of activities to ensure their economic viability, as well as trying to retain familar architecture and settings for more sentimental reasons. As Sigfried Giedion, the author of *Space, Time and Architecture,* wrote as early as 1955: 'In the 1920s one was forced to do away with nineteenth-century tendencies, when one had to begin from scratch. Today the situation is completely different. We stand at the beginning of a new tradition. One need no longer destroy what the preceding generation accomplished, but one has to expand it ...'

Britain can learn from similar trends which have been taking place overseas. The west coast of America, San Francisco in particular, provides several examples of how districts can be revived by a process of renewal. In 1962, William M. Roth purchased the former Ghirardelli chocolate factory in San Francisco, built between 1893 and 1916. He was determined to show that his native city could be improved without destroying the best from its past, and that it was a sound investment to adapt historic architecture to new job-creating uses. Lawrence Halprin & Associates, urban designers, together with Bernadi and Emmons,

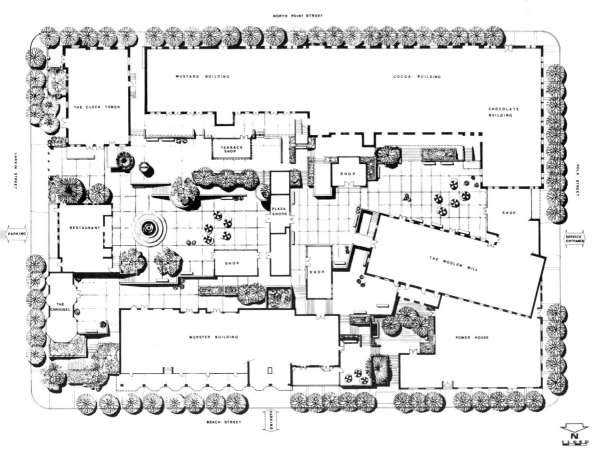

architects, transfomed the waterfront buildings into 75 retail shops, 16 cafés and restaurants, and a theatre. By 1979 it was providing employment for 800 people.

This experiment, which had paid such handsome dividends, was repeated a few years later (by Joseph Esherick Associates) at the Cannery, another converted factory in San Francisco; and at Faneuil

Faneuil Hall, Boston, which became the highest turnover shopping centre in America after its conversion.

Hall Market, Boston. Faneuil Hall became the highest-turnover shopping centre in America, grossing more than one and a half times its nearest competitor and attracting 12 million visitors a year. In each place, speciality shops and places to eat and enjoy oneself gave rise to what has been called 'leisure shopping', that is, shopping for non-essentials.

In London it is the revival of riverside warehouses in the former dockland areas of the Thames that has become one of the great success stories of the re-use of old buildings. Prices of £200,000 and £300,000 are not uncommon for flats with river views in these converted buildings. Among the earliest entrepreneurs to move in was Andrew

Thameside warehouses, now without a commercial role, are being converted into flats. This is New Concordia Wharf.

At first, the appearance of antiquity may have served chiefly to make innovation respectable; the English genius for changing content without changing form, for innovating under the cloak of continuity, has often been praised, but as time went on, more and more stress was put on the antiquity of form than on the novelty of content. The carapace, and fascination with it, became an increasingly tighter bond upon the life within.

MARTIN J. WIENER
English Culture and the Decline of the Industrial Spirit 1850–1980

Wadsworth, who persuaded the development company which owned New Concordia Wharf to sell it to him. A Victorian warehouse built in 1885, New Concordia Wharf is situated on the south bank of the river, east of Tower Bridge, and took its name from Concordia near Kansas City, from where Seth Taylor, an importer, had bought much of his produce.

Wadsworth always wanted a mixed development, and in 1981 received planning permission for 60 flats of different shapes and sizes, 20,000 sq. ft of workshops and studios, 3,000 sq. ft of offices, 3,500 sq. ft of restaurants, a riverside swimming pool, a jetty, games room, communal roof garden, caretaker's flat, laundry room, and a basement car park. The architects Pollard, Thomas, Edwards & Associates restored what they could. When introducing new elements, such as staircases, they used nautical details which they had studied at St Katharine's Dock across the water. Wadsworth moved on to St Saviour's Dock nearby and developed the Courage Brewery site by Tower Bridge. On neighbouring Butler's Wharf, 11 acres of run-down warehouses are being restored by entrepreneurs Sir Terence Conran, Jacob Rothschild and Lord (Alistair) McAlpine.

Not all the people living in these warehouses are in the upper income bracket. The London & Quadrant Housing Trust, for example, has converted Thames Tunnel Mills at Rotherhithe into flats for single

people and young couples by gutting the interior and rebuilding around a central, top-lit seven-storey atrium with balcony access to a roof garden. What the tenants like is the character and individuality of each of the warehouses, and of course, the views. One occupant said: 'For the first few days we just couldn't stop looking out of the window. Your view is forever changing – boats and what have you going up and down, and London all around you. It's lovely.'

Older properties are also being converted and developed for commercial uses. Hay's Wharf, opposite the Tower of London, is being redeveloped as London Bridge City, and includes Hay's Galleria, which will be roofed over like a Victorian arcade while retaining the existing walls of the adjoining Cubitt warehouses of 1850. The glazed tunnel opens on to the river, giving public access to the river frontage.

Inevitably in conservation, matters are never cut-and-dried, and some compromises have to be made. St Katharine's Dock by Tower Bridge is often cited as an example of how east London and Dockland can be 'opened up' and some of its old buildings re-used. While it is generally agreed to be a successful venture – as a World Trade Centre, shops, and an hotel – much of Thomas Telford's architecture was replaced.

Other warehouses and factories from the country's industrial and trading past are proving to be adaptable to new uses. Albert Dock, for example, in Liverpool, is the country's largest collection of Grade I

Left and *right*: **A top-lit seven-storey atrium with balcony access and a roof garden form the central feature of Thames Tunnel Mills.**

Modern architecture has added to our language and had a useful if puritanical purging effect, but its rejection of the status quo and therefore history alienated the movement from cities and urbanism. It is in this area where it has most clearly failed.

TERRY FARRELL
Terry Farrell
Architectural Monographs (1984)

Hay's Galleria, formed by roofing over neighbouring Cubitt warehouses of 1850 as part of the London Bridge City redevelopment.

listed buildings, and was under threat of comprehensive redevelopment for many years. After their closure in 1971, there were even plans to fill in the dock basins for use as car parking, but in 1984 the first phase of an ambitious £100-million regeneration scheme began. Eventually it will house offices, shops, museums and flats as well as providing the 'Tate Gallery' of the North.

A similar scheme has brought new life to Bristol's docks – unusual in that they are situated in the heart of the city. West India Dock on the Isle of Dogs in London is likely to be transformed into a shopping and leisure area by the Rouse Corporation, responsible for Faneuil Hall Market in Boston and similar conversions in New York. And in Chatham's historic dockyards in Kent, a £300-million plan proposes to create, over ten years, a 150-acre business park, 80 acres of museum, and 1,000 new houses and flats.

In the late 1960s came one of the great set battles between a local authority and conservation and community interests: Covent Garden. The story of how Covent Garden was saved clearly illustrated that the public could no longer be disregarded in planning matters. The Greater London Council proposed wholesale demolition of the area to make way for a six-lane motorway running parallel with the Strand.

Albert Dock, Liverpool, is the largest group of Grade I listed buildings in Britain.

In any civilisation the mannered imitation of the past, of a mock historical kind, usually means impending collapse.
ARNOLD TOYNBEE
(1852–83)

Cherries so red, strawberries ripe
At home, of course, they'll be storming.
Never mind the abuse,
You have the excuse,
You went to Covent Garden in the morning.
MUSIC HALL SONG

Some of the warehouses at Albert Dock are being converted into the Tate Gallery of the North. The docks closed in 1971.

Buildings appeal to us in different ways; our eyes may be delighted by the colour, texture and form; our intellect may be stimulated by the skilful use of materials or the brilliance of building technique; or our sense of fitness may be impressed by the excellence of the building for its purpose. In each case, however, we see revealed to us something of the living man, for no architect can give his building a finer quality than exists in his own mind.

RALPH TUBBS
The Englishman Builds (1945)

The self-appointed 'gentlemen' of the press, these senile young men and aged adolescents, best-preserved preservationists, conservationists, antiquarianists and retrogrades of all sorts, grounded in reaction, drug us into the morass of induced nostalgia, ignoring the rhythm of today.

But fetishism of the past is in reality but a lack of confidence of the future, and a fear of rupture with the safely familiar. These arbiters of trivial values, the fake quasi-neo's, dream of a mass return to a distant gas-lit womb.

No, I fear architects will search in vain for enlightenment or inspiration from that quarter.

BERTHOLD LUBETKIN
RIBA President's invitation lecture (1985)

Shops in the £100-million regeneration of Albert Dock, Liverpool.

Taking its name from the gardens of a convent which had stood on the site, Covent Garden had opened as a fruit and vegetable market in the late 1640s. But with the relocation of the market south of the Thames, the fate of Charles Fowler's 1830 building seemed doomed. Then, in the early 1970s, local residents and traders decided to make a stand and oppose the council over its plans. They formed the Covent Garden Community Association, with elected street representatives. Such was the power of public opinion that, following a public inquiry, the then Environment Secretary, Geoffrey Rippon, effectively scuppered the grandiose concept of roads, conference centre and hotels by listing more than a hundred buildings.

Not only was the Covent Garden saga a defeat for planners' planning and a victory for local people; it also marked one of the first full-blown public-participation exercises in Britain, in which the professional

A view of Covent Garden Market as it was in c. 1890. (Compare with colour photograph on p. 33.)

The car is the greatest problem for architecture.
WALTER GROPIUS
The Sunday Times (1960)

Buildings should be good neighbours.
PAUL THRIRY
quoted in *Contemporary Architects* (1980)

experts had direct access to and daily contact with real clients, the users of their work.

Covent Garden had escaped the fate of the market at Les Halles in Paris, which was destroyed and for many years remained just a large hole in the ground. Armed with the slogan 'Covent Garden belongs to the people', it became the capital's first Action Area for improvement. Since 1974 the GLC has spent £24 million on property acquisition and development, including building 500 new flats locally; £4 million went on restoring the market buildings.

Covent Garden is now one of the most lively and distinctive areas of London, with new businesses established in retailing, entertainment and catering, generating nearly £2 million a year in rental income (at 1985 prices) and drawing four million visitors a year. Speciality shops have been introduced: arts and crafts, antiques, books and prints, fashion and accessories, plants and flowers, gifts, delicatessen and retail food, toys, wine bars, restaurants, pubs and cafés. Busking and street theatre are positively encouraged – Samuel Pepys recorded that he first saw Punch and Judy performed there in 1662 – and neighbouring buildings have found new uses: the Old Flower Market, for instance, has become the London Transport Museum.

Many towns in northern England, the victims of the long-term decline of British manufacturing industry, are emulating these pioneering schemes in Liverpool, Bristol and London. One example is the restoration of the Piece Hall in Halifax. This monument to the pre-Industrial-Revolution cloth trade was once used by handweavers, who sold their 'pieces' of cloth from small shops set into galleries around a courtyard. Having since been used as a fruit and vegetable market, the local authority spent £300,000 on converting it into a community centre with craft shops, an industrial museum and a tourist information centre. It was re-opened in 1977.

To justify and enhance their superior status, architects feel called upon to make impressive statements. Consequently to speak in such circles of conservation and modest infiltration can be to evoke a kind of castration complex of the sort that afflicts an army when it has to hand in its arms.
LIONEL BRETT, VISCOUNT ESHER
Parameters and Images:
Architecture in a Crowded World (1980)

Although conservationists in Britain have asserted themselves with some success, they do not win all their campaigns. British Rail, which in 1945 owned almost 6,000 stations, now has less than 2,350, and seems to be at constant war over its tally of 600 listed buildings. George Gilbert Scott's masterpiece of St Pancras, bitterly attacked when it was built, was scheduled for demolition in the 1960s. However, it was soon listed Grade I and converted into offices. In 1977, the then chairman of the British Rail Board, Sir Peter Parker, publicly committed the nationalised industry to conservation, and set up an environment panel which included two architects. Yet a 1984 skirmish to save Francis Thompson's and Charles Trubshaw's Derby Station was lost. Derbyshire Historic Buildings Trust, having saved the neighbouring nineteenth-century railway cottages, failed to save the station. In its place is a modern station with, says SAVE, 'all the qualities of a suburban hypermarket.'

Between 1960 and 1978, manufacturing employment across Britain dropped by as much as 27 per cent. But, as Dr Nicholas Falk argued in a

lecture to the Royal Society of Arts in 1984, 'The real problem ... is not that of making the physical conversion to new uses and roles, but of making the mental changes needed to manage decline in ways that are acceptable to all concerned. This is largely due to the inertia and conservatism of the institutions that control the bulk of the resources, and their unwillingness to recognise the significance of the post-industrial age we are entering.' Nineteenth-century textile towns, with vast multi-storey mills, ship-building areas with huge sheds, now empty, and more recent industrial estates, are all prime cases for treatment.

Over the past 10 years or so, Dr Falk and his company URBED (Urban and Economic Development) have learnt that short-term strategies using indigenous resources have far more chance of bringing about long-term success than more ambitious schemes which run a high risk of failure. He calls his approach Balanced Incremental Development (or BID). A start is made where it is easiest by building on existing resources that are under-utilised, and removing the most damaging defects. The BID system aims to provide buildings which both appeals

Right: The Brunel project in Rotherhithe, celebrating the world's first underwater tunnel.

Opposite top: The old Derby station, which conservationists unsuccessfully tried to save from demolition.

Opposite bottom: The architects' model of British Rail's new Derby station. 'All the qualities of a suburban hypermarket,' said Save Britain's Heritage.

DESIGNER OF THE FIRST UNDERWATER TUNNEL IN THE WORLD FROM THIS VERY PLACE

BRUNEL
SIR MARC
1769-1849

to outsiders and also benefits the existing community, so that there is a balance. The four typical phases of a BID strategy are: providing work spaces for small firms; improving the surroundings (necessary to create confidence); building housing for sale; and creating commercial facilities.

There are many parallels between the industrial north of England and New England in the United States, where the Bank of Boston carried out a study which stressed the importance of historic mills 'in facilitating the recovery and accommodating the growth of the region's high technology industries'. Although the main users were traditional industries reborn in declining areas, a quarter of new jobs, and two-thirds indirectly, were accounted for by new technology industries; half the new technology firms were accommodated in what had at some stage been old mill space.

Dr Falk pointed out that of 550 cotton mills in Lancashire which closed between 1951 and 1961, two-thirds were in use again by the end of that period. Even in Oldham, which had had 40 per cent of Britain's cotton spindles in 1900, most of the mills had now been turned to new industrial use. An analysis by URBED showed that in the mid 1970s, 32 of the 75 mills had been re-used for manufacturing, 8 for warehousing, 6 for small industrial or workspace units and 5 for mail-order warehouses. Only 9 were vacant or had been demolished. But new developers and development trusts are constantly needed to bring about the necessary changes, to protect the resources of buildings, and to create new employment, finding common interest between public, private and voluntary sectors in new partnerships.

Just such a partnership has been formed at Sowerby Bridge, near Halifax, Yorkshire, where two local councils and private firms in the town and Government agencies have put together a proposed £6-million scheme to restore and revive a group of derelict mills dating from the late eighteenth to the early twentieth centuries. The 3-acre site on the River Calder provides in a range of industrial, commercial and recreational facilities. Its intended uses are comparable with Dean Clough, Britain's largest Victorian mill – more than a mile long – in the centre of Halifax.

This was bought in 1983 by Ernest Hall, who took just three hours to decide upon the purchase. He has converted 1 million sq. ft of space into a base for 95 small firms and a workplace for 500 people. 'This place was fraught with possibilities,' he said. He spent £1 million on the job, but has produced a commercial return while charging only £1 per sq. ft rental (in 1985). Services covered by that charge include informal business advice; for an additional charge, on-site secretarial services, a conference room and Calderdale Business Exhibition Centre are available. Tenants include manufacturers, craftsmen, caterers and computer firms.

A similar property is Lister's Manningham Mill in the northern town of Bradford. Designed by Lockwood and Mawson, and built on a scale

Manningham Mill, Bradford, looking for a new role as workshops and offices for small businesses or conversion to residential use.

comparable to many American New England mills, it is the most spectacular of the Yorkshire mills. Marcus Binney, president of SAVE, compared its two parallel ranges without a centrepiece to the Uffizi of Florence, and the chimney–campanile to that in St Mark's Square, Venice.

The mill's exterior was cleaned in the early 1970s during the 'Operation Eyesore' campaign. By 1977 its working population had declined from 4,000 people to only 600, all working in the ground-floor weaving sheds. An enterprising suggestion by SAVE proposed moving the Victoria and Albert Museum's Indian Collection into Manningham Mills for the benefit of the large Asian community in Bradford, but that idea foundered. Converting it to residential use is the obvious alternative, but by 1985 no entrepreneurial saviour has appeared. Perhaps a trust similar to the one set up in the small town of Wirksworth, 14 miles north of Derby, could ensure a future for problem buildings like Manningham. At Wirksworth, a 3-year regeneration experiment was carried out, achieving increased job opportunities, higher investments in shops, development of the local tourist industry and better care of older properties, thus reversing the town's decline over the past hundred years.

Other countries have followed the example of America and Britain in preserving their building heritage, adapting it and ensuring its future. A notable case in Dublin is the recent conversion of a hop store by Arthur Guinness into a Museum of Brewing, a Guinness visitor centre, art

A commitment to conserving historical memories and patterns adds immeasurably to our lives and the arguments for their demolition on the grounds of 'progress' are quite indefensible; if technology can do so much, it should be able to conserve with ease what there is left of the past. If technology is to add to our lives, then a route via destruction cannot be justified because it impoverishes us.
TERRY FARRELL
'British Architecture After Modernism' in *Terry Farrell*
Architectural Monographs (1984)

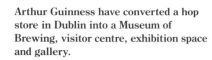

Arthur Guinness have converted a hop store in Dublin into a Museum of Brewing, visitor centre, exhibition space and gallery.

Engulfed by so much residual evidence of history, a real problem does exist for the British of reconciliation of past with future but the challenge of this conflict gives direction and real architectural opportunity. There are differing views of the past and different weighting given to what remains, but the only genuinely uncreative interpretation is that which argues that the collective memory needs to be erased in order to progress – to recommend denial is, as even Hollywood cowboys remind us, 'running away from oneself'.

TERRY FARRELL

'British Architecture After Modernism' in *Terry Farrell* Architectural Monographs (1984)

Stop this useless longing for the past. Pass by, we are working for the future since the threads of history are in our hands!

GEORGE BERNARD SHAW

gallery and exhibition space by the local firm of Scott Tallon Walker. The store was built in the 1870s on the site of the older Greene's Sugar Bakery, with 3-in.-thick pine-plank floors spanning 6 ft between joists, rolled-steel beams and cast-iron columns, under a timber- and iron-trussed slate roof. It has now been sensitively refurbished to reveal the intrinsic qualities of the unpretentious, utilitarian structure and adapted with care to its new function.

The northern mill towns of France are in some respects ahead of Britain in adaptation of their historic buildings for residential and community use. Specialists in this field are Reichen and Robert, a Paris architectural practice which has carried out several mill conversions, the best example being perhaps at the Blin et Blin cotton mill project at Elbeuf in Normandy. One of the partners, Philippe Robert, describes their approach as involving conservation and 'enhancement' of the original character although, 'the last thing we want to do is carry out an Ancient Monument exercise.' At Elbeuf, Robert attempted to reinterpret certain elements of the industrial architecture and to re-use the existing structure and decoration.

The upper floors of the mill have been made into public housing, with shops on the ground floor and a youth club in the former massive boiler room. It has been executed with conviction and has proved to be good value for money for the local authority and French Government which backed it. As a result of the conversion, the people of Elbeuf have not had to adjust to a major disruption of the familiar urban scene, and a reassuring continuity has been preserved.

But the view that conservation is beginning to prove that it is economically viable is not one universally shared. Martin Pawley, Architecture Correspondent of the *Guardian*, interviewed in 1985, remarked, 'I think the grip that conservation has got over a built environment can only be loosened by the operations of the economy itself. This is only because I believe that what conservation requires is something that it is economically impossible for this country to provide. A good analogy, I think, is with a life-support system for a very aged patient. Now, people are designed to stay alive more or less until the age of 65. After 65, it starts to be a job to keep them alive. After 95, you require all the resources of modern science; this really is what happens to old buildings. They have a designed life, and they are subjected to various ageing processes. If you try to push them beyond that, you spend a very great deal of money doing it.'

Still, it is almost inconceivable now that as recently as the mid 1960s a large area of Whitehall seemed likely to be obliterated so that new Government offices could be built, that in the 1940s Alfred Waterhouses's Manchester Town Hall was scheduled to make way for a motorway, and that Scott's St Pancras Station was under threat until protected by listing.

There can be no doubt that the conservation movement has generated enormous interest in many aspects of our architectural heritage

and vernacular building tradition, and is having a profound influence on architects designing new buildings. The current concerns, for buildings which are 'contextual' (i.e. they relate to their immediate surroundings), for refurbishment rather than for replacement, and for the re-introduction of pattern, colour, decoration and ornament, are all ones which help close the gap between architects and the population at large.

The examples of vernacular revival in such recent buildings as Andrew Derbyshire's Hillingdon Centre and Building Design Partnership's Ealing Centre in London are really a continuation – after a 50-year lull – of the English Arts and Crafts Movement. And the Classical revival, as practised by Quinlan Terry, Robert Adam and John Simpson, is in part a reaction against the banality and blandness of so much recent building. Through their interest in conservation and traditional design, the public have given their verdict about the deficiencies of modern architecture. Architects are now begining to respond to their views.

St Pancras railway station and hotel, George Gilbert Scott's masterpiece, was scheduled for demolition in the 1960s before being converted into offices and listed Grade I.

Hillingdon Civic Centre, perhaps a spin-off from conservation interest, is Neo-Vernacular architecture on a grand scale.

republics, when man has dreamed of ideal places he has also dreamed of them inhabited by ideal societies.

Thomas More coined the name 'Utopia' for his book of 1515, describing his vision of an ideal society, from the Greek meaning 'no place'; indeed there was no model for the place he described. Robert Owen's New Lanark experiment in the late eighteenth century was one idealistic blueprint for building a new world; such concepts also concerned nineteenth-century thinkers like Charles Fourier, Henri Saint-Simon, Ebenezer Howard and William Morris. For Morris, Utopia lay in a re-interpretation of a medieval society and its architecture, which he fostered by his Arts and Crafts Movement, and described in his 1891 fantasy *News from Nowhere*.

But by the twentieth century, the urban totalities which had been foreseen had become purely mechanistic and technological. The philosophy was epitomised by Frank Lloyd Wright in a lecture of 1901, when he referred to 'the greatest of machines, the city'.

Antonio Sant' Elia (1880–1916), the Italian Futurist, gave his version of the shape of things to come in his *Messagio* of 1914:

'We must invent and rebuild *ex novo* our Modern City like an immense and tumultuous shipyard, active, mobile and everywhere dynamic, and the modern building like a gigantic machine. Lifts must no longer hide away like solitary worms in the stairwells, but the stairs – now useless – must be abolished, and the lifts must swarm up the facades like serpents of glass and iron. The house of cement, iron and glass, without carved or painted ornament, rich only in the inherent beauty of its lines and modelling, extraordinarily brutish in its mechanical simplicity, as big as need dictates, and not merely as zoning rules permit, must rise from the brink of a tumultuous abyss; the street, which, itself, will no longer lie like a doormat at the level of the thresholds, but plunge storeys deep into the earth, gathering up the traffic of the metropolis connected for necessary transfers to metal cat-walks and high-speed conveyor belts . . . We must begin by overturning monuments, pavements, colonnades and flights of steps, by submerging streets and squares, by raising the level of the city, by altering the earth's crust to reduce it at last to serve our every need, our every whim.'

His vision became reality, in part, in the megastructures of Le Corbusier, which others misinterpreted to form the urban nightmares of the post-war era; in the proposed Walking Cities of Archigram and the infinite boxed structures of Archizoom and Superstudio circling the globe; in *Metropolis* and the city-planet of Trantor in Isaac Asimov's *Foundation*. Significantly, perhaps, Le Corbusier described his buildings as 'laboratories' in the retrospective of his work from 1929–34. Are we to conclude that the animals used in his experiments are human?

The rationality of science was seen to be the key to the future. As Cedric Price put it, 'The answer is technology – now what is the question?' But what may now appear to be the search for simplistic solutions was a response to genuinely felt desires to improve the human

The town is compassed with a high and thick wall, in which there are many towers and forts; there is also a broad and deep dry ditch, set thick with thorns, cast around three sides of the town, and the river is instead of a ditch on the fourth side. The streets are very convenient for all carriage, and are well sheltered from the winds. Their buildings are good, and are so uniform, that a whole side of a street looks like one house. The streets are twenty feet broad; there lie gardens behind all their houses; these are large but enclosed with buildings, that on all hands face the streets; so that every house has both a door to the street and a back door to the garden.
THOMAS MORE
describing the city of Amaurot in *Utopia* (1515)

We must ask the bat-eyed priests of technology what on earth they think they are doing.
LEWIS MUMFORD

Architecture requires us continually to reinterpret and revalue technology in human and social terms.
SIR PHILIP DOWSON
Contemporary Architects (1980)

Alone in a centrally-heated, air-conditioned capsule, drugged, fed with music and erotic imagery, the parts of his consciousness separated into components that reach everywhere and nowhere, the private citizen of the future will have become one with the end of effort and the triumph of sensation divorced from action. When the barbarians arrive they will find him like some ancient Greek sage, lost in contemplation, terrified and yet fearless, listening to himself . . .
MARTIN PAWLEY
The Private Future (1973)

A scene from Fritz Lang's film, *Metropolis* (1926), one vision of the city of the future.

. . . after all, architecture is an art and from time immemorial it has been regarded as one of the greatest. Beautiful buildings, the Parthenon for instance, Chartres, or St Paul's have moved men more profoundly than any but the very greatest masterpieces of painting and sculpture: but who is going to be moved, except by resentment, by buildings such as Herr Mendelsohn produces or M Le Corbusier in France, or by buildings of steel and brick that purport to be made of concrete, buildings cased in steel and glass, buildings that appear to follow no principle but that of contradicting everything that has ever been done before? I suggest that our modernists are wrong in principle.
REGINALD BLOMFIELD
Architect (1932)

The future must be comfortable and can be more comfortable by the juxtaposition and regard of every type of hardware and software. We should not shy at using science along with myths, engineering along with atmosphere, movement in a counterpoint with enclosure and solitude.
PETER COOK
quoted in
How to Play the Environment Game
(1973)

A bicycle shed is a building; Lincoln Cathedral is a piece of architecture. Nearly everything that encloses space on a scale sufficient for a human being to move in is a building; the term architecture applies only to buildings designed with a view to aesthetic appeal.
NIKOLAUS PEVSNER
opening lines of
An Outline of European Architecture
(1943)

lot. As Alison Ravetz wrote of the nineteenth-century radicals and revolutionaries in *Remaking Cities*: 'From the imposed blueprint it was a short step to environmental determinism – the use of physical planning to dictate a certain kind of society or to "solve" social problems – and this was a device that fitted perfectly the "clean-sweep" attitudes of planning.'

The American poet–philosopher–engineer, R. Buckminster Fuller, had as his axiom 'More with Less' (cf. Mies van der Rohe's 'Less is More') which he put into practice in a series of projects starting with the Dymaxion House ('Dymaxion' = 'dynamic' + 'maximum efficiency') of 1927. This was much more a 'machine for living in' than anything designed by Le Corbusier. It was an assemblage of mechanical services and living areas, a theme again taken up in his Wichita House of 1946. This lightweight, prefabricated bungalow was built of two hundred components which could be delivered to site in a stainless-steel cylinder no bigger than a typical American motor-car. If produced in volume, each home would cost just $3,000.

The aircraft industry, Fuller believed, had many lessons for the traditionally conservative building industry, and indeed this second house design was commissioned by the Beech Aircraft Corporation. But of more lasting influence was his geodesic dome design, which reduced the amount, weight and waste of material needed for shelter to the absolute minimum whilst giving maximum enclosure. The potential for military use at remote bases was quickly perceived. In a startling proposal of 1955, Fuller suggested a two-mile hemispherical dome for Manhattan, providing a completely controlled environment. It would cost around $200 million, but this would soon be repaid in savings to the

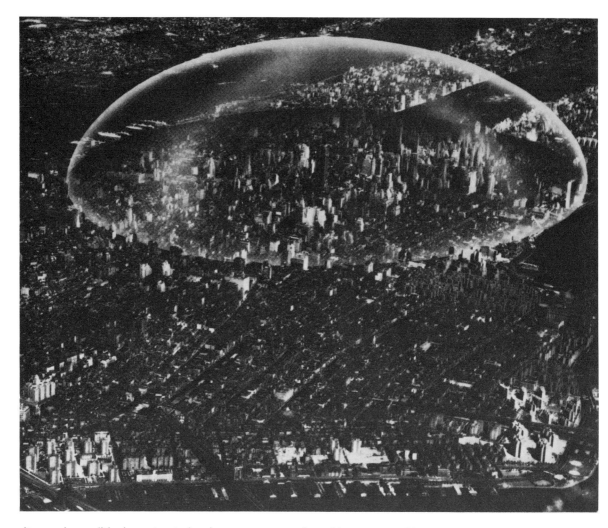

city on air conditioning, street cleaning, snow removal, and lost man-hours from colds and respiratory ailments.

Such a concept was greeted as techno-romantic imagery on a super-scale, but he was not alone in this. Since 1970, Paolo Soleri, an Italian-born visionary much influenced by Frank Lloyd Wright (for whom he worked) and by Antonio Gaudí, has been building his city of the future in the Arizona desert. Arcosanti is the dream inspired by Soleri's philosophy of 'arcology' ('arcology' = 'architecture' + 'ecology'), a multi-level industrial city first envisaged by Tony Garnier (1869–1948), who published his designs for Cité Industrielle in 1917, but transferred to a remote location. Unlike Frank Lloyd Wright's Utopia, Broadacre City, where each family would live on an acre of land to practise an independent, isolated lifestyle based on individual freedom, Soleri's is stacked up to 25 storeys and covers just 10 acres to house up to 5,000 people involved in co-operative effort. Compact design, making it more likely

More and more people want to determine their own parameters of behaviour. They want to decide how they shall behave, whether it's playing, working, loving, etc. People are less and less prepared to accept imposed rules and patterns of behaviour. Doing your own thing is important.

People are becoming more interested in people and reality, rather than in feeding mythical systems. Unfortunately, however, in terms of doing your own thing, architecture is clearly not working.
MICHAEL WEBB and DAVID GREEN
Archigram

A two-mile-diameter hemispherical dome for Manhattan, proposed by Buckminster Fuller c.1955.

Each step we make today toward material progress not only does not advance us towards the general well-being, but shows us, on the contrary, that all these technical improvements only increase our miseries.

TOLSTOY

The reasonable man adapts himself to the world; the unreasonable one persists in trying to adapt the world to himself. Therefore all progress depends on the unreasonable man.

GEORGE BERNARD SHAW
Man and Superman

Meanwhile if these hours are dark do not let us sit deedless like fools and fine gentlemen. Rather let us put our workshop in order against that great day when there is an art made by the people and for the people as a joy for the maker and the user.

WILLIAM MORRIS
'The Arts of the People'

that people will meet one another and feel part of a community, is Soleri's main concern in the design, unlike Fuller's adoption of efficiency as the prime determinant. People will live in close proximity to where they work and play; each area will be carefully designated. Food will be produced artificially in the bowels of the mega-city, apart from what can be grown in the surrounding landscape. Bicycles will be the only form of transport. The design is an act of faith in urban living just when so many towns and cities in Western countries are becoming depopulated as people choose to move out to the suburbs. New York City has a density of 33 people per acre; Delhi, 72; Arcosanti is intended to pack 215 people to the acre.

Arcosanti is probably still twenty years or more from completion, being constructed largely by students who pay for the privilege of building it. It is an experiment in self-sufficient urban living. It anticipates the day when the oil runs out.

Cars are banned and personal relationships – at the settlement – count for more than the received imagery of the media (there will be no technological communication either). It rejects the commercial values of the city in favour of the creative energy of men and women; for the time being, at least, it promotes a monastic lifestyle of dedicated hard work, with tobacco and alcohol also prohibited.

But Soleri has greater visions, more imaginative and more ambitious still. These include Novanoah I, a 6,800-acre floating city–home for 400,000 people living off the oceans; Stonebow, a bridge joining either sides of a canyon and housing 200,000 over 316 acres; Hexahedron, two crystalline pyramids rising 3,500 ft into the air with 170,000 people at 1,200 to the acre; and Asteromo, a 70,000-population spaceship cylinder.

Soleri brushes off descriptions of himself as dreamer, lunatic or genius. He prefers to think of himself as a realist. His Utopia takes built form but does not presuppose a social pattern. He says he designs cities, not societies: 'I only build the instruments. I do not write the music.'

Architecture, as architects never cease to remind us, is a social art. The design of buildings both profoundly influences and reflects the nature of the society around it. So if we are to consider how architecture might develop, we must simultaneously examine where modern society is progressing.

In the early 1960s, in the south-west of the United States, many chose to 'drop out' of conventional society and pursue alternative lifestyles. One of its first manifestations was Drop City, a settlement near Trinidad, Colorado, where three former students of the University of Kansas bought a few acres of goat pasture and started to build. Their model was Fuller's geodesic dome. Over the next few years a number of structures sprang up as recorded by the commune's chronicler, Peter Rabbit. Their materials were the by-products of the industrial and materialistic society they had left behind: scrap timber, car windshields,

waterproofed tar paper, all of them painted sky blue. It was a rejection of the high technology and consumerism in an age of abundance; self-sufficiency was one of the main attractions for its followers.

These early gestures did not perhaps have fully thought-through philosophies: were it not for the industrial society which they reject, there would be no waste material to use!

But not only did the original 'Droppers', as they called themselves, set a pattern which found many imitators, but a whole industry of alternative living sprang up, with its own bible, the *Whole Earth Catalog*.

Its preface said that a new age was dawning in which 'intimate personal power . . . [the] power of the individual to conduct his own education, find his own inspiration, shape his own environment' was the path to salvation.

Sometimes the spiritual anxiety and search for new meaning found expression in such religious communities as Findhorn, in the north of Scotland, where a New Age settlement grew up.

In American cities, Paul Davidoff was developing the idea of advocacy planning.

This was a system by which minority groups within urban societies were given more autonomy, and could plead their special case for their

A 'Dropper' at Drop City, Colorado, begun in the early 1960s by three former students of the University of Kansas.

If there were dreams to sell
What would you buy?
THOMAS LOVELL BEDDOES

The mental process of foresight is one of the essential bases of civilisation. It is both the source and the means of all undertakings, whether they be large or small; it is also the assumed basis of politics.
PAUL VALÈRY
Oeuvres (1957)

When a man has obtained those things which are necessary to life, there is another alternative than to obtain the superfluities; and that is, to adventure on life now.
HENRY DAVID THOREAU
(1817–62)

Aristocracy links everybody, from peasant to king, in one long chain; democracy breaks the chain and frees each link.
ALEXIS DE TOCQUEVILLE
(1805–59)

The health of a democractic society may be measured by the quality of functions performed by private citizens.
ALEXIS DE TOCQUEVILLE (1805–59)

The most difficult advance is back to reason.
BERTHOLD BRECHT

Too many people spend too much time looking back with regret and forward with fear that they fail to realise the present is there offering them flowers.
CHINESE PROVERB
Quoted by Michael Manser, President of the RIBA, in a letter to the *Sunday Telegraph* (27 January 1985)

So leap with joy, be blithe and gay,
  Or weep, my friends, with sorrow,
What California is today,
  The rest will be tomorrow.
RICHARD ARMOUR

own interests against those of others. Participatory democracy was given a new lease of life. Changes in family living patterns, encouraged by greater personal mobility and affluence, allowed the concept of communities of interest – as opposed to ones based on physical constraints – to flourish.

But while the various alternatives being practised in hundreds of small groups in different countries were for the most part unstructured, a number of loosely related factors brought about a different way of looking at the world and how people might live in the future.

As material wealth spread to wider levels of society – at least in Western countries – so the ultimate futility of measuring success by acquiring ever more goods became apparent to more and more people. Materialism gradually began to be overtaken by a concern for such things as 'quality of life'. Counter-cultural views became absorbed in conventional wisdom.

Writers such as Lewis Mumford, Ivan Illich, and Fritz Schumacher started to challenge traditional assumptions about Western society, providing a broad context in which to discuss the sort of responsive environments that were needed. Architecture would have to be part of that responsive environment. *Europe 2000,* edited by Peter Hall, published in 1977, made some specific predictions for the decade of the 1980s. Some of the key trends identified by Hall's international committee were as follows:

— a period of successive economic crises; insecurity brought on by increasing competition from the Third World for resources and markets; dissatisfaction with assembly-line production and the dawning of a post-industrial age;

— increasing alienation, particularly among the young, who have less materialist values and want a fulfilling life;

— home and family becoming less important as other networks of association and support develop;

— polarisation of society between rich and poor;

— conservation of resources;

— growth of intermediate technology with tools which liberate the individual and allow him better to work at shaping his own environment and life pattern, in contrast to machines which enslave the individual to labour for money;

— growth in the number of smaller working groups at the expense of larger organisations [this prediction seems accurate: details about architectural practices in Britain, released in 1985, for example show that almost half the profession of 27,000 are now in practices employing just one or two people];

— decline in the proportion of new buildings as refurbishment and renewal increases;

— growth of service industries at the expense of manufacturing ones.

Much of this tallies with Alvin Toffler's prediction (in *The Third Wave,*

1980) of a home-centred society working from its 'electronic cottages':

'This implies less forced mobility, less stress on the individual, fewer transient human relationships, and greater participation in community life . . . The electronic cottage could help restore a sense of community belonging . . . If employees can perform some or all of their work tasks at home, they do not have to move every time they change jobs, as many are compelled to do today. They can simply plug into a different computer.

'The transfer of work, or any part of it, into the home could not only reduce energy requirements but could also lead to energy decentralisation. Instead of requiring highly concentrated amounts of energy in a few high-rise offices or sprawling factory complexes, and therefore requiring highly centralised energy generation, the electronic-cottage system would spread out energy demand and thus make it easier to use solar, wind and other alternative-energy technologies. Small-scale energy generation units in each home could substitute for at least some of the centralised energy now required . . .

'Some businesses would shrink in such a system, and others proliferate or grow. Clearly, the electronics and computer and communications industries would flourish. By contrast, the oil companies, the auto industry, and commercial real estate developers would be hurt . . . We cannot today know if, in fact, the electronic cottage will become the norm of the future. Nevertheless, it is worth recognising that if as few as 10 to 20 per cent of the workforce as presently defined were to make this historic transfer over the next 20 to 30 years, our entire economy, our cities, our ecology, our family structure, our values and even our politics would be altered almost beyond recognition.'

These trends suggest profound changes too in the type, number and form of buildings of the future. When the economic life of a building is generally taken to be at least 60 years – so that those now on the drawing board or computer plotter in 1985 can still be expected to serve a useful function in the year 2045 – then likely changes in society need close examination.

Market research studies are tending to confirm Toffler's scenario. A leisure and lifestyle survey conducted in Britain by Mintel in 1984, for example, showed a population slowly becoming more home-oriented, with expenditure up on home entertainments (this includes home computers) and do-it-yourself materials, largely due to the increase of home ownership, up from 42 per cent in 1980 to 61 per cent just two years later. Leisure time spent at home increased from an average of 30 hours per week in 1939 to 45 hours a week in 1984, due in part also to shorter working hours.

A grass roots economy is springing up as people move from dependence to post-industrial self-reliance. Barefoot economists are convinced that mass unemployment and the help being given to small local ventures are forcing Britain, America and other Western nations towards the new age. Even the large corporations are slimming down

Architecture means the thoughtful housing of the human spirit in the physical world.
WILLIAM O. MEYER
Contemporary Architects (1980)

Most city diversity is the creation of incredible numbers of different people and different private organisations, with vastly different ideas and purposes, planning and contriving outside the formal framework of public action. The main responsibility of city planning and design should be to develop – insofar as public policy and action can do so – cities that are congenial places for this great range of unofficial plans, ideas and opportunities to flourish, along with the flourishing of the public enterprises.
JANE JACOBS
The Death and Life of Great American Cities (1961)

Oh, how much depends even for the best of men upon the time in which he was living.
Inscription on the tomb of
Pope Hadrian VI, Rome

We are now at the close of one epoch and well before the start of a new one. During this period of transition there will be no moratorium on building, and for obvious reasons. There will just be more architecture without architects.
PETER BLAKE
architect and critic (1974)

*Indolent people with a vested interest in
the* status quo *reject rational enquiry in
case they find out too much, since reason
leads to understanding, understanding
exposes injustice, and injustice calls for
dreaded change. Thus reason is rejected
not because it failed us – but out of fear
that sooner or later it might succeed.*
BERTHOLD LUBETKIN
RIBA President's invitation lecture
(1985)

by hiving off whole departments, whose staff regroup to form independent suppliers of goods or services. Among the prophets of such
developments was Leopold Kohr, whose book *The Breakdown of
Nations,* published in 1957, gave Fritz Schumacher the central idea for
Small is Beautiful, published in 1974. And in 1984, James Robertson,
the 'anti-economist', outlined his vision of the SHE economy – Sane,
Humane and Ecological. As the *Guardian* pointed out: 'The essential
revolution is personal: decolonise yourself. "Think globally, act locally,"
is one of its few slogans.'

Architects have themselves contributed to speculation about the
possible future. Roy Mason, an American architect who specialises in
energy-conscious structures, foresees that 10 per cent of all homes will
have some type of alternative energy system, such as solar or wind
power by 1990. By 1992, 40 per cent will have some form of home
computer – the 'house brain' – which will control information, entertainment and energy-management systems. There will be telecommunication, telebanking and teleshopping. By 1996, he suggests, it will be
possible to buy an add-on room or a totally self-contained living unit to
plug into your existing home. By 2005 large-screen 'video walls' will
provide media texture so that you can 'dial an environment and surround
yourself with the Grand Canyon, Taj Mahal or other imagery space'. By
2015 environments could be responsive to one's mood in terms of light,
sound and colour.

Similarly, Dr Marvin Adelson, a professor in the department of
architecture and urban planning at the University of California, Los
Angeles, and a founder of the Institute for the Future, believes that
many homes will generate enough energy to feed into the grid when
they have surplus. Major new urban projects will mix previously separated zones of activity (work, home, leisure) around shopping malls or
California-style 'security communities' with their own management
providing services, such as policing and parks, normally paid for out of
taxes. Wealthy people will move back into the city centres as run-down
areas are revived, and some of the poor will be provided with ownership
in return for the rehabilitation of old properties and neighbourhoods.
Educational training programmes, plus advice and counsel from the
building professions and trades, will provide these 'new pioneers' with
the necessary skills. Adelson adds, cautiously, that 'the match between
transitional architecture and transitional social structure will not always
work out well for the people concerned'.

Computers will help architects to try out their designs before they
ever get built, says Dr Adelson, and aid them in meeting numerous
demanding performance specifications. These will include energy conservation, the living pattern of each occupant, aesthetics, cost, materials, components and the detailed construction process required. 'To
the extent that these possibilities are actually realised in practice,
architects will provide suitable, individualised buildings for human uses
of all kinds, and a much greater proportion of buildings will reflect the

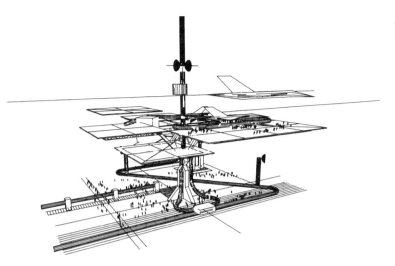

A computer-drawn airport of the future by D. Y. Davies and Associates.

benefits of an architect's participation.' Here it is worth noting that in Britain fewer than 40 per cent of all buildings are at present architect-designed, and in America even less.

Julie Rivkin, director of Chicago computer operations for the architectural firm of Skidmore, Owings and Merrill, designers of many of the largest buildings in the States, including the world's tallest skyscraper, the Sears Tower, explains that computers can help the designer to visualise better in three dimensions, at any scale. They can help unravel intricate details of construction, save weeks of drawing-board time when something is changed, help to come to better decisions more quickly on matters like floor plans and areas, or the best colour and texture of elevations, and test impact on the surroundings by, for example, predicting shadows which will be cast. 'It just happens to be a fairly sophisticated type of design tool', she states, 'because of its three-dimensional design capabilities, and its speed and accuracy.'

'We don't replace the human touch at all, however,' she adds. 'I think it would be a mistake to think about computer-aided design in that way.'

What can we expect to be the key features of the house of the future? Typically it will have a number of energy-saving features, which might together save up to half of what we now consider as 'normal' energy consumption. It will also have computer-based home management information and entertainment systems. New lifestyles will require more rather than less space, and may require greater adaptability of buildings as changing family needs demand provision for work at home, 'granny annexes' and larger individual rooms for teenagers. With this there will be the need to ensure more privacy by good planning and sound insulation. It may well be in Britain that instead of knocking through party walls in adjoining small cottages, the most suitable adaptations could be of Victorian and Edwardian terrace houses, and even of semi-detached houses of the inter-war years.

It was only with the advent of central heating that the whole house

Progress sometimes sets you backwards.
SAN DIEGO AIRLINE CLERK
referring to the losing battle he was fighting against
a new computerised booking system
quoted by Michael Davie in
In the Future Now (1972)

came to be used simultaneously. The kitchen has replaced the living-room hearth as the centre of communal life. In due course, the conservatory is likely to usurp the kitchen, since it is a practical extension which is a passive solar heatstore in the winter and a cooling vent in summer. David Turrent, an architect and partner in Energy Conscious Design, a London firm, believes the house of the future will be much better insulated and will need less energy because of both passive and active solar heating.

A bold experimental building designed by Turrent's firm was the BBC Television *Money Programme* Future Home in the new town of Milton Keynes. It has a large conservatory to heat the whole house. That alone saves up to 2,000 kiloWatt-hours a year (the average British 3-bedroom semi-detached house uses 25,600 kWh/yr), which if multiplied nationally across several thousand new homes could significantly reduce the country's energy bill. As Turrent says: 'As the cost of supplying gas from the North Sea fields increases, and the price of domestic gas escalates, then low-cost solar water heating will become much more attractive during the 1990s.' At present it is the artificially low price of gas to the consumer which still makes it financially unattractive in Britain. Another experimental house built for a television programme was Granada's 'House for the Future', converted from an old coach-house in Macclesfield, Cheshire; it proved just how adaptable older premises can be to new ideas.

Milton Keynes has been at the forefront of low-energy housing in the United Kingdom, where about 200 new houses of this type have been

Energy-cost savings of at least 30 per cent should be achieved at Milton Keynes Energy Park, started in the early 1980s.

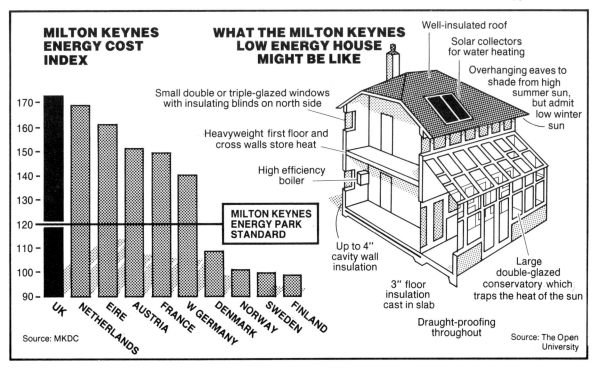

MILTON KEYNES ENERGY COST INDEX

Source: MKDC

WHAT THE MILTON KEYNES LOW ENERGY HOUSE MIGHT BE LIKE

Well-insulated roof
Solar collectors for water heating
Overhanging eaves to shade from high summer sun, but admit low winter sun
Small double or triple-glazed windows with insulating blinds on north side
Heavyweight first floor and cross walls store heat
High efficiency boiler
MILTON KEYNES ENERGY PARK STANDARD
Up to 4" cavity wall insulation
3" floor insulation cast in slab
Draught-proofing throughout
Large double-glazed conservatory which traps the heat of the sun
Source: The Open University

built over the last five years. The town has recently launched a £100-million Energy Park, where energy cost savings of at least 30 per cent should be achieved. Typical three-bedroom houses built to current UK building standards have an energy cost index (ECI) of 173, compared with 150 in France and about 100 in Scandinavian countries. The target at Milton Keynes will be 120. The architects behind the idea hope that the index will be widely adopted so that house buyers will be able to compare them on estate agents' particulars along with service charges and rateable values.

At the end of its seven-year development period the Energy Park will be home to more than 3,000 people. It will cover 300 acres and provide 2,000 jobs in similarly designed low-energy factories and workplaces. The planning and orientation of the buildings, road layout, shelter-planting and landscaping will all contribute to the overall energy plan.

We should learn from the snail: it has devised a home that is both exquisite and functional.
FRANK LLOYD WRIGHT
quoted in the *Guardian* (1959)

A development at Great Linford, Milton Keynes, completed in 1981 and monitored by the Open University with funds from the Department of Energy, demonstrated that additional capital expenditure of just £350 per house produced energy savings of £120 per year (at 1981 prices), a payback period of less than three years. The energy saving features were:

— low cost plastic-framed double glazing;
— insulation 3 ft wide around the edge of the ground-floor concrete slab;
— 4 in. of cavity wall insulation (rather than the normal 2 in.);
— 5½ in. of loft insulation (normally 2 to 4 in.);
— draught-proofing to all external doors and windows;
— a high-efficiency, low-thermal-capacity boiler, wall-hung and with a sophisticated control system.

The total cost of these items was £500 per house, but savings in the cost because of a smaller boiler and the positioning of radiators away from windows, thus reducing the length of pipework, reduced the cost increase. Further savings could have been made by insulating the whole ground-floor slab by the addition of a south-facing conservatory to catch the sun's radiation and provide low-cost living space, and by adding a small solar water-heating system.

Microprocessor technology is becoming widespread in the home. This will monitor energy consumption and heating in each room, pro-grammable up to a year in advance. Multiplied to a national scale, savings created by such precise control will be substantial.

Such technological progress has direct consequences for domestic architecture. Speculative house-builders, who are responsible for more than two-thirds of all new homes built in Britain at present, are starting to recognise the commercial advantages of the Milton Keynes type of property; buyers are attracted by cost-saving design providing the house looks conventional and is not like past experimental houses which have appeared as 'freaks'.

The design of workplaces, too, is likely to improve in the years immediately ahead, making them more enjoyable places; as more firms opt for decentralisation, moving away from expensive city-centre locations, this starts to become more practicable. In 'greenfield sites', it is possible to arrange for new buildings to draw energy from combined heat and power schemes (CHP), using some of the otherwise waste energy from power stations, which are only some 33% efficient. The other 67% is normally dissipated to the atmosphere, or used to warm fishponds at the base of cooling towers. The principle is not new: Churchill Gardens, the 1946 housing development in Pimlico, was designed to use waste heat from Battersea Power Station. But the concept was not widely used. However, such CHP systems are now common in Europe and America, and in theory up to 30 per cent of Britain's domestic and commercial heat could be supplied in this way.

Expert energy managers should be appointed to carry out audits on consumption and suggest ways to reduce it, both in space heating uses and in industrial processes. It has also been proposed to set up neighbourhood Energy Action Projects (similar to Housing Action Areas) and Energy Advice Centres modelled on the Citizens' Advice Bureaux and Legal Aid schemes already in operation at local level.

The Centre for Alternative Technology at Machynlleth in Wales was founded in 1975 and in 1985 was still the only community in the world living solely off solar, water and wind energy. It aims to make it all comprehensible to the general public. It drew half a million visitors to its remote location in a disused slate quarry in the first 10 years: a practical

A solar wall is incorporated into staff cottages at the Centre for Alternative Technology at Machynlleth in Wales.

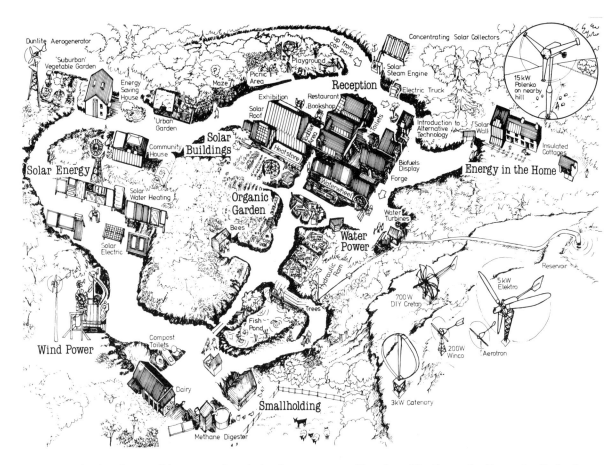

example of what is possible, even though its lessons are still only grudgingly taken seriously by government. Peter Raine, its director, describes it as 'a relic of the spirit of the Sixties', perhaps more concerned with a certain amount of naive idealism than the harsh realities now facing us. But it has raised public consciousness of the issues with such publications as its 1977 *An Alternative Energy Strategy for the United Kingdom*. And the British Government has at last grasped part of the nettle, possibly motivated by a desire to reduce expenditure rather than out of any environmental concern for the future of non-renewable energy sources.

In declaring 1986 to be Energy Efficiency year, Peter Walker, Secretary of State for Energy, said: 'I do not know of any other sphere of the British economy where we can save £7 billion so easily.' The intention was to move Britain to the top of the energy efficiency leagues by 1990.

'The next decade will see some of the most rapid and far-reaching changes in the history of architecture', predicted the Worldwatch Institute's 1980 paper on *Energy and Architecture: The Solar and Conservation Potential*. Yet this requires a fundamental change of approach on the part of architects and designers, who have, at least

The Centre for Alternative Technology is the only community in the world living solely off solar, water and wind energy. It was founded in 1975.

The great Puritan experiment to discover the limits of human capacity for taking punishment has not benefited mankind as expected. Anybody who is able to perceive the wretchedness of our way of life and the containers who shape it will want to strive for a more dignified existence. The difficulty lies in finding a way out of our mental slump.
BERNARD RUDOFSKY
The Prodigious Builders (1977)

until the mid 1980s, largely ignored climate, the orientation of buildings, and the idea of massive structures to act as thermal banks. They have preferred instead to rely on the 'artificial respiration' of heating and cooling systems, expensive to instal and even more expensive to run. It is not only architects' attitudes which need to be changed: some countries' tax regulations discourage energy-efficient building. Britain, for example, allows companies to write off running costs against tax but not capital costs; such an anomaly should also perhaps have been encompassed in the Energy Secretary's strategy.

British architect Bryan Avery believes that innovation using technology as a useful tool, rather than as 'the engine of destruction of social and environmental values,' can provide many solutions to current problems. He points out that industry in Britain is moving out of city centres into suburbs and countryside, encouraged by the swing to service industries. Toffler's predictions have proved very accurate: in 1950, 40 per cent of the workforce was engaged in manufacturing; in 1985, the figure was only 26 per cent; employment in the service sector has grown from 43 per cent to 65 per cent in the same period. Shopping is also moving out of town to larger and larger centres, often now with several multiple stores combining their range of goods at the same location.

The city then, deprived of primary industrial and commercial activity at its core, can be rebuilt for family housing at very high density. It is a return, in concept, to the Georgian and Regency grand-scale terraces, crescents and squares, with housing four or more storeys high. Belgravia, Bayswater and Bloomsbury in London, or Bath, Brighton and Leamington Spa all provide examples. But the new kind of terrace house would be for all, not the well-to-do who have always inhabited areas like these.

Avery has devised a high-density, high-technology form of terrace house, which has as its key a lift driven by a linear induction motor developed by the Otis Elevator Comapny. The house is designed for maximum space-saving and for very low maintenance. It is equipped with advanced electronic control and energy management systems. The result is a multi-storeyed, narrow-frontage home with its own front door, private and sound-proofed, of single aspect. It could easily back on to other types of buildings, whether shopping centres, warehouses, factories, office blocks or sports facilities. Zoning would be done away with. Cities would once again be multi-use, multi-occupation places. Derelict land – of which there was 176 square miles in England alone in 1982 – would once again become useable when not arbitrarily zoned inappropriately.

The concept was awarded a commendation in the 1985 UNESCO/Tsukuba architectural competition, 'Tomorrow's Habitat'. The architect has since developed the idea further for suburban and countryside applications.

Although such housing may have widespread applications, it is also

Not only is ornament produced by criminals but also a crime is committed through the fact that ornament inflicts serious injury on people's health, on the national budget and hence on cultural evolution.
ADOLF LOOS
Ornament and Crime (1908)

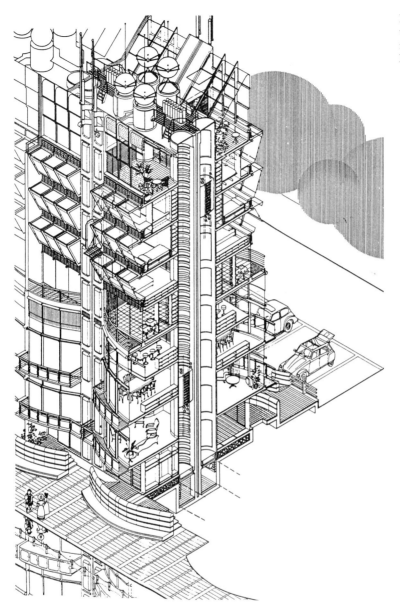

Bryan Avery's high-density, high-technology housing with linear induction lifts developed by the Otis Elevator Company.

adaptable to varying immediate surroundings. But another method of working *with* rather than *against* the natural environment has been the increasing use of earth-sheltered buildings, whether they simply employ a sod roof or are constructed completely beneath the surface of the earth. Earth is a natural insulator that reduces temperature fluctuations in both winter and summer. By providing such structures with south-facing glass walls, the sun's heat can be effectively collected and stored in the same way as in lean-to conservatories added to low-energy homes. Earth-topped roofs have the additional advantage of

All work passes out of the hands of the architect into the hands of nature, to be perfected.
HENRY DAVID THOREAU
(1817–62)

Perhaps the blank faceless abstract quality of our modern architecture is a reflection of the anxiety we feel before the void, a kind of visual static which emanates from the psyche of us all, as if we do not know which way to go.
NORMAN MAILER
Cannibals and Christians

The future is not what it used to be.
GRAFFITO

Williamson Hall, at the University of Minnesota, has deciduous vines which control direct sunlight in summer and allow it to enter the building in winter.

providing natural evaporative cooling in the summer, something which has made them popular in countries like America and Israel. In these climates, watering the roof might be the only air conditioning necessary. The main constraints on their wider use until now have been the high cost of building underground and the difficulty of making such environments attractive places for people to live and work in. Norway and Switzerland build many general-purpose buildings underground as part of their civil defence policy, but there are many instances of acceptable environments being created. In Australia, for example there are several subterranean mining villages, and in China, where there has been continuous occupation of underground space for thousands of years, latest estimates suggest that as many as 20 million still live in this way.

'Earthscrapers', as they have inevitably been called, are now home for about 5,000 American faimiles, while in Oklahoma there are 27 subterranean schools. But because of the high cost, there must be good reason to burrow out a home. Most of the earth-sheltered homes are in the central States, between Minnesota and Texas, which have extreme weather, including tornadoes. Expensive land, severe planning controls (the need to 'hide' away a building) or the prior claims of agriculture on precious flat land in mountainous regions are also reason enough.

David Bennett, professor of architecture at the University of Minnesota, explains that 'although you may have a temperature swing of 130 °F, from 100 °F in summer to −30 °F in winter, you can maintain a steady 55°F through the natural insulation of the earth if underground.' Williamson Hall, on the University campus, is a two-storey structure,

26 ft deep, built underground because there was insufficient space above ground for a building large enough for the 50,000 to 80,000 people who use the facilities at any one time. The problem of bringing in light is overcome by having an open triangular courtyard at the centre of the building. Deciduous vines control direct sunlight in summer and allow it to enter the building in winter.

The Civil and Mineral Engineering Building has a core space of 50,000 sq. ft, 110 ft down, a specification determined by natural geology. The Underground Space Centre is built in a rock cavern of about the same depth. In this, the temperature variation is less than one degree Fahrenheit between extreme seasons, even while 130°F at the surface. Ray Sterling, its director, explains that the $12-million complex of offices, lecture theatres and laboratories has the world's largest periscope – called an ectascope – to pipe street scenes and light down below.

In Minneapolis, the Seward town houses have heating bills one-third to one-quarter those of a conventional house of the same size and shape in the climate there. The houses are built behind and beneath a bank of

Above: The interior of Williamson Hall is much like that of any other modern building, even though it is partially submerged underground.

Opposite top: Rockefeller Plaza, New York. Summer day and winter night. See p.71.

Opposite: Brooklyn Bridge and Manhattan. The romantic silhouette of Brooklyn Bridge leading into a Manhattan skyline created by the pressure of space, and consequent high land values. The two towers, nearly 1,600 ft apart, rise 272 ft from the water. Design work began in 1869; the Bridge was opened in May 1883.

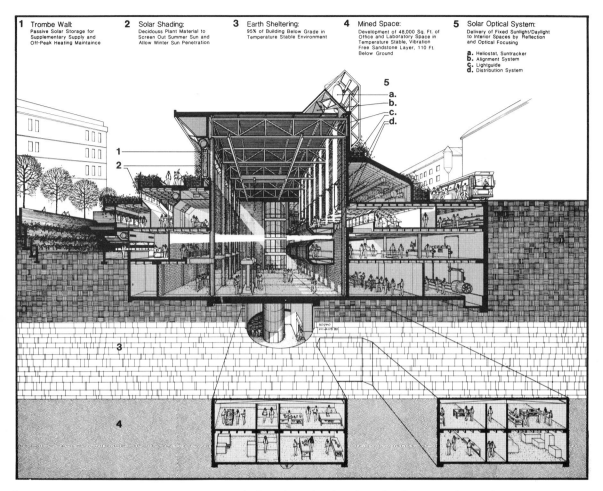

1 Trombe Wall: Passive Solar Storage for Supplementary Supply and Off-Peak Heating Maintaince

2 Solar Shading: Deciduous Plant Material to Screen Out Summer Sun and Allow Winter Sun Penetration

3 Earth Sheltering: 95% of Building Below Grade in Temperature Stable Environment

4 Mined Space: Development of 48,000 Sq. Ft. of Office and Laboratory Space in Temperature Stable, Vibration Free Sandstone Layer, 110 Ft. Below Ground

5 Solar Optical System: Delivery of Fixed Sunlight/Daylight to Interior Spaces by Reflection and Optical Focusing
   a. Heliostat, Suntracker
   b. Alignment System
   c. Lightguide
   d. Distribution System

The Civil and Mineral Engineering Building at the University of Minnesota has a core space of nearly 50,000 sq. ft, 110 ft below ground level.

Opposite: **PPG Place, Pittsburgh. Architecture as corporate identity: Philip Johnson and and John Burgee created soaring Gothic spires in glass as appropriate imagery for the headquarters of the Pittsburgh Plate Glass Company in Pennsylvania. The client had been impressed by the Palace of Westminster in London, built 1835–60 in stone.**

earth, largely to deaden the noise from an adjacent freeway. But on the opposite side, the south, there are large areas of glazing and solar collectors, to make use of the sun's energy. The houses are built in concrete, itself a good thermal store, and have insulating shutters which are closed at night in the winter to store and re-radiate the warmth collected during the day. Underground homes are now a cult following in America, with a magazine, *Earth Shelter Digest,* and manuals, such as *The Underground House Book,* for enthusiasts.

Apart from the civil defence bunkers beneath Whitehall and dotted around the countryside as regional seats of government in time of war, the only earth-sheltered building of any note yet completed in Britain is a house designed and lived in by the architect Arthur Quarmby. Underhill, in the Yorkshire village of Hulme, was finished in 1975 and has uphill rooms facing a swimming pool beneath a large transparent dome, and downhill rooms with a magnificent view of the Pennines in which it sits. Many hillside towns and villages nearby are partly cut into slopes, but Quarmby sees the current interest in underground dwellings as part of a

All that is visible above ground of Arthur Quarmby's house, Underhill, in the Yorkshire village of Hulme.

tradition which stretches back to the 'black houses' or 'soddies' of the remoter parts of northern and western Scotland and the west coast of Ireland, where buildings were lost in the landscape. Part of the attraction for him is the dramatic contrast between light and dark spaces internally, but he also points out that if the current level of submerging the countryside in concrete and tarmacadam continues, then in two hundred years' time the country will be covered from John O'Groats to Land's End.

In 1985, the British Department of Environment started to examine the possible use of exhausted mineral working for earth-sheltered buildings – for industrial and commercial as well as residential use. Such buildings can be sited in areas of outstanding natural beauty where no conventional structures would be contemplated. The Department of Energy approved Quarmby's 1984 design for a house for Stuart Bexon,

Stuart Bexon working with David Robertson and Arthur Quarmby on the design of his underground house at Westonbirt in the Cotswolds.

at Westonbirt, Gloucestershire, in the Cotswolds. The four-bedroom house is 15 ft below ground, with a 32-ft circular glass-covered courtyard and swimming pool at the centre of the eggshaped plan. Planning permission for a conventional house was refused for the green-belt site. Bexon has found that he can use cheaper materials for several elements of the house, so the cost is no greater than for a conventional one, and he will probably save 80 per cent on his fuel costs. It is so energy-efficient, in fact, that he will be able to grow plants all year round, as in a greenhouse. Ray Sterling and other American architects visited during construction to see work progress and proffer advice. The British Earth Sheltering Association was founded in 1983, an indication of growing interest in such structures.

Left: A model of the School for New Woodland Industries, at Hooke Park, Dorset, which started on site in the summer of 1985.

Right: Architect Richard Burton, on site at Hooke Park.

A series of structures at Hooke Park, Dorset, also pays more than lip service to ecology and the need to fit in with the environment. Architects Ahrends, Burton & Koralek, working with engineers Ted Happold and Frei Otto, are responsible for a woodcraft school for furniture maker John Makepeace. It is built of trees felled from the surrounding forest, generally of unsuitable quality for building. The timber is being left unseasoned, though treated against rot, used 'wet' as the main

structural material in tension, and infilled with greenhouse-style glazing. A PVC-coated polyester fabric is used for the outer roof membrane, turfed to camouflage the workshop and residential blocks, and
coated with mossy gravel on the central tent of lecture theatres.
Richard Burton describes this use of poor timber which would otherwise be pulped or burned as 'a wonderful breakthrough and a new
tradition in construction'.

The transition from a reliant society to one which is more self-
sufficient has also manifested itself in new methods of architects collab-
orating with the communities in which they live and work. The term
generally applied to it is 'community architecture', although a debate
about semantics, and the involvement of other environmental professions, has given rise to alternatives such as 'technical and environmental
aid', and 'social architecture'.

In community architecture people are directly involved in managing
the buildings and environment in which they live or work as well as
commissioning and designing a scheme with help from a local architect.
The extent to which the users of the buildings participate can vary from
consultation to full control, and it operates at many different scales,
from the individual home to the planning of entire neighbourhoods.

The keys to its success are the 'disaggregation' of the scale of the
project (small is beautiful); the devolution of power to a residents'
association, tenants' group or town trust; and giving people access to
professional advice, which may be a local-authority architect or private
consultant living and working in the same community as his clients, the
users of his building.

A fundamental change has come about in the role of the architect; he
is no longer a *provider* but an *enabler,* helping people to help themselves.
He has more concern for the *process* of building than the final *product,*
although that, too, is often superior in quality as a result of involving
users. The barriers against this new approach – such as paternalistic
professional attitudes and political dogmatism – are gradually being
overcome. In community architecture, architects are 'expert friends' of
the client, rather than 'hired consultants', or, worse, the 'anonymous
doctors' they appear to be when members of ever-changing teams of
'public' design offices.

The idea of creating an environment directly responsive to people's
social and cultural needs and aspirations is intended to reinforce personal identity and a sense of community, which have been almost
entirely absent from most mass-housing schemes built since the end of
the Second World War. The underlying thesis is that the environment is
better if those who live, work and play in it are involved in creating and
managing it. The community architecture movement is now national
and international in scope, with parallel developments in America,
Europe and in the developing countries of the Third World, such as the
South American *barriadas* (makeshift self-build communities). Its
advance signifies a return to the former pattern of patronage where

Citizen control
Delegated power
Partnership
Placation
Consultation
Informing
Therapy
Manipulation

SHERRY R. ARNSTEIN, 'A Ladder of
Citizen Participation in the USA', in the
*Journal of the American Institute of
Planners* (July 1969), reprinted in the
*Journal of the Royal Town Planning
Institute* (April 1971)

*I know of no safe depository of the
ultimate powers of society but the people
themselves: and if we think them not
enlightened enough to exercise their
control with a wholesome discretion, the
remedy is not to take it from them, but to
inform their discretion.*
THOMAS JEFFERSON (1743–1826)
US president (1801–9) and Architect

*What I find most interesting about the
new range of architectural heroes is that
they are thought important for the
process rather than the product. It is the
way they go about their work which
excites rather than the formal qualities of
their work . . . When Jim Johnson took
me to the original ASSIST shop in the
Govan Road, everybody in the street
greeted him with a smile. Does this
happen to the local authority architect
inspecting an improvement area?*
COLIN WARD
(1978)

accountability is to client–user, rather than to the local council and bureaucracy (in the public sector), or to stockholders and boards of directors (in private developments).

Pioneers in community architecture were architects such as Jim Johnson of ASSIST in Glasgow, Ralph Erskine and Vernon Gracie in the Byker area of Newcastle; Jim Monahan in Covent Garden, London; and Rod Hackney in Macclesfield, who has become the movement's most skilled politician and propagandist.

Community architect Rod Hackney with residents of the Black Road II General Improvement Area in Macclesfield.

How cartoonist Louis Hellman, of the *Architects' Journal*, saw Hackney's role in helping the self-help builders of Birmingham.

Hackney set up the Black Road Area Action Group in Macclesfield in 1972 to fight the council's demolition plans for a group of early-nineteenth-century terrace cottages. He won, then set about implementing the first self-help General Improvement Area scheme in the country, with residents doing much of their own building work. His office was a corner shop in the road, two doors down from his own house. At the time he called it 'only working-class conservation', but further schemes followed, with another group of houses in Black Road, and in rehabilitation work in Birmingham, Cleater Moor and Millom in Cumbria, Leicester, and with self-build housing for those on the council waiting list in Stirling, Scotland.

The mid 1980s saw between five hundred and a thousand community architects at work in Britain. The movement was supported by the Royal Institute of British Architects in 1976, when it set up a working group on the subject, and in 1982 for the first time it was given a small amount of financial support by the Department of the Environment. Hackney sees community architecture's future as being a national service, in the same way as the National Health Service and Legal Aid.

What brought community architecture to national attention outside the architectural world was the speech given by the Prince of Wales to architects at Hampton Court Palace in May 1984, when he said he thought it important because it showed 'ordinary' people that their views are worth having, 'that architects and planners do not necessarily have the monopoly of knowing best about taste, style and planning, that they need not be made to feel guilty or ignorant if their natural prefer-ence is for the more "traditional" designs.' Hackney was singled out for praise, along with architect Ted Cullinan, for designing buildings which are 'beautiful as well as socially useful'.

In February 1985 the Prince paid a private visit to Macclesfield to see for himself what was achieved and to discuss with those involved in bringing it about the merits of a community architecture approach. He returned to the same theme at the Institute of Directors' annual con-vention at the Royal Albert Hall in London, shortly after his visit, which had also included the Liverpool new-build housing co-operatives, another example of architecture at work for the benefit of the whole community.

Speaking of his visits he said: 'I was electrified by the atmosphere I encountered. In the case of the Liverpool co-operatives, the residents had been living in slum clearance areas and were due to be dispersed throughout the city by the council. With the help and expert advice of their own architect, they fought their way through the seemingly impenetrable entanglements of red tape and official opposition until they finally succeeded in building the houses *they* wanted in the kind of layout they liked.

'They were now responsible for the maintenance of their properties and that fact alone has virtually eliminated the vandalism that was previously so rife. The intimate involvement of the community in the

It's a strong community now where we live, because we've made it so with doing the work we have done to our houses. At one time, I only knew my next door neighbours or the people that shared the yard with us. We spoke to the other people – just 'Hello' and 'Good morning', but now it's 'Are you coming over for a cup of tea?' Everybody's friendly and it's really brought us close together as a community.
JUNE DANIELS
Chairman of the Black Road Residents' Committee, interviewed on BBC Radio Four (April 1979)

God helps those that help themselves.
THE MAYOR OF MACCLESFIELD
on the completion of the Black Road I General Improvement Area (1975)

What I believe is important about Community Architecture is that it has shown 'ordinary' people that their views are worth having; that architects and planners do not necessarily have the monopoly of knowing best about taste, style and planning; that they need not be made to feel guilty or ignorant if their natural preference is for the more 'traditional' designs – for a small garden, for courtyards, arches and porches – and that there is a growing number of architects prepared to listen and to offer imaginative ideas.
HRH THE PRINCE OF WALES
addressing architects
at Hampton Court Palace (1984)

The Prince of Wales visits Rod Hackney's Black Road II scheme, in Macclesfield, on 8 February 1985, shortly before his speech to the Institute of Directors.

The most important thing about it is the power to the people bit. In general, in Liverpool people are told what they are getting, not asked what they want. But once we had established our viability by being accepted by the government for funding, we determined everything; the way we lived, and who we employed to run our affairs. We did not succumb to bureaucracy.

We got the architects and builders and everybody else on our terms. We told them what we wanted and consulted right the way through, from day one, at every stage. Through the design committee we decided on every single aspect of the scheme right down to the sort of trees we planted.

We've proved to the council and government and anybody else listening that if people are given the reins, get the right help and are committed, they can come up with a really excellent viable housing scheme that people want to live in.

ALAN HOYTE
First chairman of
Hesketh Street Co-operative, Liverpool
(1984)

design of its houses has ensured that character, individuality and taste have been restored . . .

'It seemed to me that if only we could enable more people to develop this kind of self-confidence in the sort of places of which most authorities and agencies tend to despair, that self-confidence, from the discovery of previously hidden talents and abilities, could spill over into other regenerative enterprises . . .

'The secret, then, lies in the simple business of allowing the "ordinary bloke" to express his views and preferences and to realise the very considerable potential which exists in so many people. However, very little can be achieved without effective management and without the professional acting as an "enabler".'

'Enablers' were prominent in the rehabilitation of Lea View House, Hackney, in east London. Before a tenants' association was formed for its improvement, no fewer than 90 per cent of the tenants had wanted to leave this hard-to-let, run-down 'sink' estate of 300 flats. Architects Hunt Thompson Associates used a community approach to good effect. A project team of four architects moved on to the estate, and managed to establish a good working relationship after years of mistrust of the council. Like the Byker office of Ralph Erskine, their office in flat number 3 soon turned into the social focus for tenants, who were involved in all stages of carrying out the four-year, £6.5-million con-

Community architects from Hunt Thompson Associates 'enabled' the residents of Lea View House in Hackney to have the sort of improvements they wanted to their homes.

tract. The lesson it provided for John Thompson, who led the team, was that the best thing for all architects and probably all other professionals was to 'get out of our ivory towers, get away from our institutes, get away from our offices, and to go out and take real people as the client, to work with real people and to genuinely serve the people.'

Some of the ideas which have evolved from participation in environmental decision-making and community architecture are now being applied to the task of inner city regeneration on a much broader scale. In June 1985 the St Mary's Street area of Southampton was the first to benefit from a visiting team of experts set up by the RIBA, called a Community Urban Design Assistance Team (CUDAT). The idea developed from the American RUDAT (Regional and Urban Design Assistance Teams) system, administered by the American Institute of Architects, devised by the (British) architect David Lewis in 1967 in response to inner-city riots. Lewis describes it as 'urban design by consensus'. What he did was to turn community participation, born of the civil rights movement, into a force for action, leading to a renaissance of inner-city neighbourhoods and reviving the tradition of local democracy in a programme of a hundred RUDATs to date.

A CUDAT is a multi-disciplinary team: in the case of St Mary's, an architect–planner, a sociologist, an economist, a traffic engineer and an administrator, under the chairmanship of architect Richard Burton. They analysed the problems of the place over a five-month period. An intensive weekend study and discussion session was then staged, with local residents, traders, planners, school-teachers and others, in order to develop a specific plan of action for its future. The positive response to the first CUDAT will ensure implementation of similar schemes elsewhere.

The last few years have also seen an expansion of self-build housing. Building societies, such a powerful force in the housing market today, began as mutual aid centres for working-class communities at the end of the eighteenth century. Groups of self-builders would save money in

The house took me and the wife 11 months to build. It was a very enjoyable experience after the time involved in getting the scheme off the ground. It is an adaptable building, unusual yes, but extremely nice to live in. The sheer joy of putting a spade in the ground. . . . Well it's an indescribable feeling . . . you finally have control over what you are doing in your life.

KEN ATKINS
Lewisham Self-Build Housing
Association (1983)

A group of self-builders in the new town of Milton Keynes.

order to buy land on which to house themselves; when the first house was completed, they would use it as security to borrow money to build the second, and so on until everyone was housed. A similar system still operates among some immigrant communities, such as the Indians and Pakistanis, in Britain.

Today self-builders are the third-largest house-building 'company' in Britain, with completions estimated at 10,000 in 1984. According to Colin Murray, secretary of the Society of Self-Builders, there are three main reasons why people go in for it:

— they want more for their money, and have definite views about the style and layout of the house they want;

— man seems to have an instinct to build for himself, to embody his ideas and labour in his home;

— the rewards, apart from the satisfaction of doing the job, should include a saving of at least 20 per cent on the mortgage required for the house and quite possibly up to 40 per cent.

Most of the homes are built by individuals, but a substantial minority are built by friendly societies. Groups register as housing associations under the Industrial and Provident Society Act, thus acquiring legal status. Each association then operates as a building company, with the cash-saving advantages of a large group. Those involved, often with the help of an architect or other building professional, might typically spend 24 hours a week over a 52-week year organising and building, including all their annual holidays. It is not something for the faint-hearted to contemplate, but banks and building societies are becoming more sympathetic in lending money, although the house must be fairly conventional if it is to be mortgaged, so as to facilitate its sale if necessary.

The counter-culture and self-help movement have come a long way in the twenty years or so since the Kansas students started to build Drop City. Even British local authorities, usually rigid and over-cautious in such matters, are supportive. Some, such as Lewisham council in south London and Milton Keynes Development Corporation in Buckinghamshire, are assisting self-builders by providing suitable land and other support. In the case of Lewisham, the council has provided full mortgages and instituted an equity-sharing scheme.

Architects are contributing too. Walter Segal, for example, has produced a sophisticated timber-frame house design so that self-builders with no previous experience could put up their homes with little more than DIY tools and a manual he devised.

Within the profession, the live issue of architecture seems to be a battle of styles: what will follow Modernism? Post-Modern Classicism, Genuine Classicism, Romantic Pragmatism, Symbolic, Hi-Tech and Late Modern are among the most widely used labels. But in the public arena, a much wider matter is at issue – the way in which people want to organise their future built environment. They are demanding a bigger say in the form and content of new buildings, so that they can identify with them and enjoy them. Buildings of the future will have to be

Doing it yourself is also instructive, practically and in arousing empathy with builders, and in that it must constitute the opposite process to the totally understandable advice that I believe Alberti gave; that the architect should never visit the site of his building while under construction, lest sympathy with the problems experienced by the builder should lead him to modify the purity of the design. In this Alberti, humanist though he was, stressed the cerebral part of the art of building; my early experience stressed the sensual or tactile.
EDWARD CULLINAN
'Building Them Yourself' in
Edward Cullinan Architects (1984)

We all see more of architecture than of any other art. Every street is a gallery of architects' work, and in most streets, whatever their age, there is good work and bad. Through these amusing shows many of us walk unperceivingly all our days, like illiterates in a library, so richly does the fashionable education provide us with blind sides.
C. E. MONTAGUE
The Right Place

One of the pavilions in Ted Cullinan's additions to Uplands Conference Centre, completed in 1984.

'What meaning does your construction have?' he asks. 'What is the aim of a city under construction unless it is a city? Where is the plan you are following, the blueprint?'

'We will show it to you as soon as the working day is over; we cannot interrupt our work now,' they answer.

Work stops at sunset. Darkness falls over the building site. The sky is filled with stars. 'There is the blueprint,' they say.

ITALO CALVINO
Invisible Cities (1974)

The danger about plans for housing is that, as its term of office ends, the present government will make gestures like the release of funds to local authorities and to the Housing Corporation in response to growing anxiety and anger over the lack of investment in housing, and that this will result in a crash programme to reassure the electors. In such programmes, the same assumptions about councils as direct providers of homes will be made, as though there was nothing to learn from the disasters of the past. Similarly the opposition will promise another version of the same plan. When we build again, we need not a plan for housing, but an attitude that will enable millions of people to make their own plans.

COLIN WARD
When We Build Again –
Let's have housing that works! (1985)

designed to be more responsive to their users. The process is one of the 'democratising' architecture.

Attitudes *do* change with time. When there were plans to demolish much of Whitehall in London and replace it with a typically gargantuan Modern Movement scheme to house government offices, common sense eventually prevailed, just as it did a century and a half ago when Augustus Welby Pugin damned Georgian architecture, in his book *Contrasts,* for being rigid and banal in contrast to the richer form of Gothic architecture! There are precedents enough for revision – or even reversal – of public taste. It is difficult to imagine the protest made about the appearance of Nash's Carlton House Terrace at the time of its construction, or to understand Jane Austen's perjorative reference to people who lived, Lord save them, in 'plain white modern houses'. There is a need for architecture to be more inventive and adventurous; to harness technology and put it to human use, rather than allow it to dictate people's lives, as it has done in the recent past.

People need to feel that they belong to their home, their neighbourhood and town: a sense of place is crucial. They also crave variety and surprise, which can be introduced by simple humanising elements such as appropriate scale, pattern, colour and decoration. A new visual language is evolving. 'There is no reason at all why architecture shouldn't be welcoming and friendly and warm and responsive, and at the same time somewhat daring and inventive,' says Ted Cullinan.

Architecture remains the most public of all the arts, and perhaps the only art that touches everybody's life every day. Its primary social purpose is to respond to people's needs and aspirations, and to bring some delight into their lives. Architects designing for the future might take a leaf out of Fritz Schumacher's book, *Small is Beautiful,* and once more practise their art 'as if people mattered'.

REALLY BAD NEWS. NIGEL'S
PASSED HIS ARCHITECTURE
EXAM.

CHAPTER SIX

THE ARCHITECTS

Most modern buildings hate people.
JOSEPH RYKWERT

Architects, along with planners (with whom they merge), intellectual disciples of Keynes and the general secretaries of trade unions, are presently prominent in the class of scapegoats, about whom nothing too harsh can be said since they are held responsible for everything which discontents us.
'Prince among architects'
Leading article in
The Times (1 June 1984)

All the public buildings of the last half century have been behind the average architectural talent of the day, manifestly because the employment has been consigned to Professional Men.
SIR EDWARD CUST MP
commenting on the controversial design of the Houses of Parliament, the subject of an architectural competition in 1835.

A doctor can bury his mistakes, but an architect can only advise his client to plant vines.
FRANK LLOYD WRIGHT

Barry Fantoni's cartoon in *The Times* following the Prince of Wales's controversial speech to architects at Hampton Court Palace in 1984.

Although the function of the architect has existed for centuries, it is only comparatively recently that the 'professional' architect emerged as an agent between client and builder. In common with other embryo professions during the nineteenth century, architects were anxious to establish their status. The prevailing view was that the architect was an artist not an engineer. Consequently the profession was largely restricted to artist–architects; the engineers, and later the other more technical participants in the building process, were excluded from membership. Understandably they formed their own representative organisations; of about thirty formally constituted 'professional' institutions today, no fewer than twenty represent the building industry.

For almost a century after the Institute of Architects was founded in 1834 as a mutual-interest society and gentlemen's club, its members shared common interests, aims, and methods, and could rely on a building industry virtually untouched by the Industrial Revolution except in the use of new structural materials. But by the early twentieth century, changes were coming about: the emergence of new building types – the involvement of architects in mass-housing estates, airports and cinemas, for example; a change in the type of client commissioning work (more 'public' works, fewer private); and in particular, the influence of the Modern Movement, sweeping in from the Continent. Those fired with its Messianic zeal saw their role as creating a new world – Utopia – through design and social engineering. That fervour was extreme, but architects generally began to appear in fresh guises, not just as individual 'artists', but as entrepreneurs and businessmen. In the 1970s and '80s, another group has emerged – community architects who see themselves neither as artists, nor as businessmen, but as 'enablers' for those traditionally unlikely or unable to employ an architect.

During the post-war reconstruction of Britain the architect found himself having to deal with bigger and broader problems such as the introduction of planning law, new methods of construction (particularly prefabrication), and new materials.

The change in client type had far-reaching consequences. Patronage used to be personal for small-scale commissions. The architect could be innovative, especially stylistically; work was often done by craftsmen using the best quality materials; and cost was not necessarily the prime consideration.

But if the patron is a corporation (from the public or private sector) with no one person making his mark on the commission, buildings often have no character or individuality; they can have none because they are not individually designed and built. There has been a rash of anonymous-looking buildings, often on a large scale; they are assembled cheaply from materials and products mass-produced for use by an unskilled labour force.

The simple relationship between client, architect and builder has been greatly altered by a system in which client, owner and end-user are no longer the same individual or company. Since the mid twentieth century, the client (say, a property development company) may be different from the owner (say, a pension fund or local authority department) and from the end user (the tenant of a speculative office block or high-rise flat). Architects are now backed up by a team of other specialists, such as quantity surveyors or cost consultants, structural, mechanical and services engineers, interior space planners and decorators, and perhaps landscape architects. Meanwhile, general contractors may be replaced by project managers (perhaps surveyors), management contractors, and an army of sub-contractors brought together for each project. Architects are spending more and more of their time liaising between these disparate groups and also trying to satisfy what they see as myopic planning officers, reactionary planning committees, an unnecessarily complicated system of building regulations (revised in 1985), intense competition over fees, and the ever-present threat of litigation if a building fails.

In addition to the professional preoccupations of architects, they are more than ever aware that, rightly or wrongly, they are held to be responsible for the appearance of the contemporary environment. As a result of some considerable pressures, architecture is in a state of some disarray, and architects themselves are uncertain about the role that they are expected to play.

They passed through a period of soul-searching in the 1970s which has now given way to a mood of realism. With commissions in the public sector in Britain down 90 per cent in real terms between 1979 and 1985, and without reflation in the private sector to take up the slack, the future is difficult to predict. Britain, with 28,000 architects, has more per head of population than any other country. America, for example, has 80,000 for five times as many inhabitants. Add to that the competition from those wanting to take on some of the architect's traditional responsibilities, plus the introduction of computer-aided design facilities, and prospects for architects in the medium term look bleak.

The same is true in North America. Harry Mileaf, a director of McGraw Information Systems and chairman of the US Co-ordinating

Most architects in practice today began their professional lives during the high tide of the Modern Movement. For 30 years after 1945 the voice of tradition was stilled and the task of the profession was to build a new world from top to bottom by means – and according to theories – of their own devising. In the 150 years of architecture now the subject of celebration, only one such era occurred. It was the time when schools, hospitals, houses, cathedrals, churches, and public buildings were erected in quantities that today already seem unimaginable. It came about for the sober reason that between 1914 and 1950 the country was at war for the equivalent of one day out of every three-and-a-half.
'Annus mirabilis 1984'
Leading article in the
Architects' Journal (9 May 1984)

The architect, as we think of him today, is a tragic hero, a sort of fallen Michaelangelo. He has built too high and has been guilty of hubris.
NICHOLAS BAGNALL
'Fallen angels'
Book review in the *Sunday Telegraph* (1983)

'The Image of the Architect' as seen by Louis Hellman, in the *Architects' Journal*.

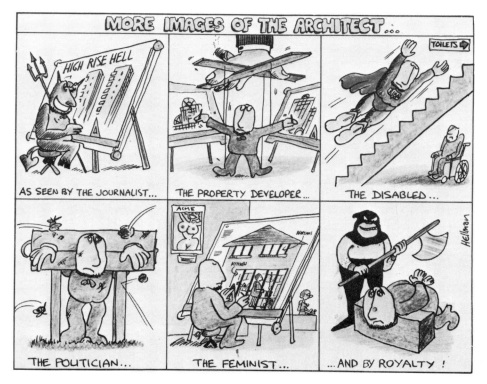

Council for Computers in Construction, warned in 1984 that by the year 2000 four-fifths of America's architects would be 'dislocated' because design in the construction process is highly labour-intensive and that work could be done better all round by computer. 'Producing architectural drawings,' he said, 'now accounts for half of all design costs for new buildings. Within 15 years, computer-aided design systems will have automated the drawing process, product specification and cost estimating.'

In Britain the education of architects is under scrutiny. Student numbers are to be reduced, and there is pressure for courses to be made more relevant to the needs of the 'real' world.

Students are still being trained to design one-off prestige projects rather than plan refurbishment schemes, repairs, and correction of defects. These smaller jobs are the bread-and-butter work for many contemporary architects, and are likely to remain so. There is also a need for more architects prepared to work in community-based practices and to carry out the massive task of helping to regenerate the inner cities.

Community architecture is the most radical alternative to conventional practice, as discussed in the Chapter 'New Directions', but although it answers a real need, it is not universally perceived as appropriate or desireable. Criticism has come even from such unexpected quarters as Ivan Illich who described it, way back in 1977, as 'this year's radical chic' and an 'enslaving illusion', in his book *Disabling Professions*.

Some years ago Sir Nikolaus Pevsner, the architectural historian, suggested that one reason for the decline in the quality of contemporary architecture lay with the quality of the client. Lacking a developed visual sense and shunning the 'unique' or the 'extravagant', he would merely require a building which combined low cost with high efficiency and bland anonymity. Better architecture, Pevsner implied, relied to some extent on having a traditional patron taking an interest in more than the most basic functions of the building. But there is growing evidence that the client at all levels is now better informed about design and environmental matters. And architects are beginning to accept – albeit reluctantly – that they should no longer impose their ideas, however 'creative' or 'imaginative', without consultation.

At a recent design conference at Eindhoven in the Netherlands the question was asked: 'If architects did not exist today, would anyone bother to invent them?' The answer is that the architect does have an important role, but that it is one which must adapt to a changing society.

In many parts of both Britain and America, it is possible to discern that architecture has become more humane, more modest, and altogether more pleasing. New housing often has decorative details which would have been absent in a design of even ten years ago. Industrial buildings of all kinds are being designed by architects of talent and imagination; it is now possible to take pleasure in the shapes and

The creative artist is by nature and by office the qualified leader in any society, natural, native interpreter of the visible form of any social order in or under which we choose to live.
FRANK LLOYD WRIGHT
(1935)

I am convinced that art, since it forms the most uncorrupted, the most immediate reflection of the people's soul, exercises unconsciously by far the greatest direct influence upon the masses of the people.
ADOLF HITLER
(1935)

The warmth and directness with which ages of crafts and a more personal relation between architect and client endowed buildings of the past may have gone for good. The architect, to represent this century of ours, must be colder, cold to keep in command of mechanized production, cold to design for the satisfaction of anonymous clients.
NIKOLAUS PEVSNER
Pioneers of Modern Design (1960)

The brazen plate upon the door (which being Mr Pecksniff's, could not lie) bore this inscription. PECKSNIFF, ARCHITECT, *to which Mr Pecksniff, on his cards of business, added,* AND LAND SURVEYOR. *In one sense, and only one, he may be said to have been a Land Surveyor on a pretty large scale, as an extensive prospect lay stretched out before the windows of his house. Of his architectural doings, nothing was clearly known, except that he had never designed or built anything; but it was generally understood that his knowledge of the science was almost awful in its profundity.*
CHARLES DICKENS
Martin Chuzzlewit

The crucial point, however, is that the lesson of modernism can now be treated as one aesthetic choice among others, and not as a binding historical legacy. The first casualty of this was the idea that architects or artists can create working Utopias. Cities are more complex than that, and the needs of those who live in them less readily quantifiable. What seems obvious now was rank heresy to the modern movement: the fact that societies cannot be architecturally 'purified' without a thousand grating invasions of freedom; that the architects' moral charter, as it were, includes the duty to work with the real world and its inherited content. Memory is reality. It is better to recycle what exists, to avoid mortgaging a workable past to a non-existent future, and to think small. In the life of cities, only conservatism is sanity. It has taken almost a century of modernist claims and counterclaims to arrive at such a point. But perhaps it was worth the trouble.
ROBERT HUGHES
The Shock of the New (1980)

The business of the architect is to make the designs and estimates, to direct the works, and to measure and value the different parts; he is the intermediate agent between the employer, whose honour and interest he is to study, and the mechanic, whose rights he is to defend. His situation implies great trust; he is responsible for the mistakes, negligences, and ignorances of those he employs; and above all, he is to take care that the workmen's bills do not exceed his own estimates. If these are the duties of an architect, with what propriety can his situation, and that of the builder, or the contractor, be united?
JOHN SOANE
Plans, Elevations and Sections of Buildings (1788)

decoration of even a warehouse or a factory. All this suggests that architecture is going through an overdue process of readjustment, one that is impelling architects to listen to what people are saying and to respond with confidence, and humour and modesty to their needs and aspirations.

The following profiles of practising architects illustrate the diversity of current approaches.

Robert Adam (born in 1948) is one of a small group of architects practising Classical Revival architecture, as in this design for a house in Salisbury.

Robert Adam
Partner, Evans, Roberts & Partners, Winchester

Robert Adam is one of a small group of architects, unofficially led by Quinlan Terry (*q.v.*), who are practising what has become known as Classical Revivalist architecture, or Genuine Classicism.

After qualifying as an architect, Adam won a scholarship to study at the British School in Rome. There he developed a particular interest in late-Classical, Romanesque, and early-Renaissance architecture. He often works in a Classical style, but also employs a broad range of historical sources.

'We have not so much revived the past as reopened the great reservoir of history,' Adam claims. Although the Modern Movement demanded that 'art shall no longer be the enjoyment of the few but the life and happiness of the masses', in fact decoration and ornament almost disappeared from architecture altogether. It is now coming back, with the Classical revival making an influential contribution.

The Neo-Vernacular style has led to an increasing awareness of the possibilities of historical analogy and has broken the spell of Modernist ideology which totally dominated the profession for so long.

No person who is not a great sculptor or painter can be an architect. If he is not a sculptor or a painter, he can only be a builder.
JOHN RUSKIN
Lectures on Architecture and Painting

Dogmersfield Park, a new computer centre for Amdahl UK by Robert Adam, has a new Baroque extension to an original Georgian house.

'The increase in the use of historical analogy is the one dominant factor in what have been called Eclectic, Revivalist and Neo-Vernacular styles. This new direction can be a bitter pill for what is, by now, the bulk of mature practising architects who have been brought up with, or converted to, Modernist theories. The unease often felt by these architects is best summarised by the frequently expressed desire to see buildings that are "of our time".'

But Adam rejects the notion of one architecture that is exclusively appropriate to contemporary society. And 'it really is a very exciting time in architecture. In fact there has not been so much ferment and fresh thinking since the 1930s.'

Adam, who is unrelated to his eighteenth-century namesake, has designed a Baroque extension to an original Georgian house at Dogmersfield Park, Hampshire, for a computer firm; a Classical end wall to a brewery in Winchester; Romanesque shops and offices, also in Winchester; and a Basilican library for the military town of Bordon, Hampshire.

Peter Ahrends
Partner, Ahrends, Burton & Koralek, London

Peter Ahrends.

Peter Ahrends has worked closely with Richard Burton and Paul Koralek since they were all first-year students at the Architectural Association in London. After qualifying Ahrends spent nearly two years working in his father's practice in South Africa before setting up in partnership with Richard Burton in London.

Paul Koralek, who won the international competition for a new library at Trinity College, Dublin, in 1961, is the third member of a partnership which has become recognised as one of the most successful architectural firms in the country. ABK's original design for the National Gallery extension was well received by the public and many critics; the revised version less so because of certain compromises. Chichester Theological College, residences at Keble College, Oxford, Habitat showrooms and offices at Wallingford, Maidenhead library and the Cummins engine

factory at Shotts, Lanarkshire, are among their completed works. A notable development is the practice's 1985 school for woodcraft industries at Hooke Park, Dorset, which uses the unorthodox material of *unseasoned* forest trimmings.

Left and **right**: Maidenhead Library, designed by Ahrends, Burton & Koralek.

Dr William Allen
Partner, Bickerdike Allen Partners, London

Patching up faulty post-war buildings is the one recession-proof sector of the construction industry today. The cost of building too quickly, too cheaply and with insufficient care and understanding has led to a bill of between £3,750 million and £5,000 million for repairing local-authority housing alone. Another survey published in 1984 suggested that a further £2,200 million will have to be spent on remedial work to private commercial property and all types of public sector projects, excluding housing, over the following 10 years.

Dr William Allen, chief architect of the Government's Building Research Station from 1953 to 1961, now acts as a trouble-shooter helping to sort out some of the problems of building defects. Several architectural-award-winning buildings have been put in his care; generally they include office and residential tower blocks, but Liverpool's Roman Catholic Cathedral of Christ the King is also among them.

Architects vary like doctors and lawyers, some are good – some bad. Unfortunately, in architecture, failure shows.
PETER SHEPHERD
former President of the RIBA

'The real generators of defects are much less obvious than poor workmanship or when design and specification are at fault,' says Dr Allen. 'The most pervasive of them is the rate of change and innovation in materials and processes which has developed since 1945. This presented learning problems well beyond the capactiy of an industry unprepared for the age of science, and with the inbuilt handicap of employing a large body of manpower of greatly varying intellectual ability. The situation was bound to become accident-prone and has done so.'

Since about 1970 the number of failures has proliferated, with condensation, leaky flat roofs and damp-proof courses, and chemical reactions in concrete. More trouble is in store, he believes, from frost damage to domestic walls with cavity insulation, and new brickwork due to recent changes in brick manufacture and the use of harder mortars.

'Myopia prevailed at senior levels in research, the industry and central administration, at a time when clear distant vision was needed. Defects were seen, for the most part, as isolated events and not the stigmata of more deep-seated problems, which is evidently their real nature.'

Dr Allen's prescription for ensuring a less troublesome future includes a continuous feedback of relevant information to the industry, and changing the thrust of architectural education so that the applied science of building rises from its present 'poverty of esteem to the realms of a modern craft skill'.

Bob Allies
Partner, Allies & Morrison, London

Bob Allies is one of the Six Young Architects whose work was exhibited in 1984 at the RIBA Heinz Gallery in London, and one of the 40 under-40 architects exhibited by RIBA in 1985. He trained at Edinburgh University and was Rome Scholar in architecture, 1981–2, at the British School in Rome, where he studied Giulio Romano's Palazzo del Tè and pursued an interest in Mannerism. He teaches at Cambridge University two or three days a week but practises in London.

A superb draughtsman, Allies shows in his work a keen appreciation of the classical language of architecture. He designed a farm at Farningham, Kent, and a competition-winning scheme for landscaping The Mound, Edinburgh (value £500,000).

'I would have liked to have seen a building commissioned to mark the Festival of Architecture [in 1984] just as the RIBA headquarters was built to mark the Institute's centenary in 1934.' He tried to organise the building of a number of structures in Hyde Park for the celebrations but ran out of time – 'we started too late, the Festival arrived too fast!'

Allies acknowledges that there is a revival of interest in Classical architecture and buildings which are sympathetic to their surroundings.

Ashley Barker
Surveyor of Historic Buildings, Greater London Council

Ashley Barker joined the then London County Council in 1959 after working for a private firm of architects where he designed shops and later prefabricated schools. He became the surveyor in 1970 and is responsible for about 1,400 historic buildings from Kenwood to Eros, and including the revived Covent Garden Market, early-eighteenth-century almshouses, and the remnants of Crystal Palace. He has to decide what alterations may be made to listed buildings in the capital, and is also responsible for the Survey of London. He employs about sixty staff, mostly architects, building surveyors, four research historians, draughtsmen and archaeologists.

'Some people say that conservation has already gone too far, but that is not my view. The views of the architectual profession and those of the public are probably different on this matter,' he says. He welcomes the activities of SAVE Britain's Heritage, the Georgian Group and other conservation lobbyists as evidence of public concern and support.

Theo Crosby
Partner, Pentagram Design, London

Theo Crosby of Pentagram, organiser of the exhibition 'How to Play the Environment Game' in 1973.

An architect and author of books on the urban environment – *Architecture: City Sense* (1963) and *The Necessary Monument* (1970) – Theo Crosby has also organised several exhibitions. By far the most important was 'How to Play the Environment Game', sponsored by the Arts Council and shown at the Hayward Gallery, London, in 1973. It is also the title of the accompanying book.

The 'game' is one of infinite dimensions, and the players – architects, planners, users of the buildings and spaces, developers, estate agents, civic societies and others – win or lose in proportion to their involvement. Decisions are constantly being made, often unilaterally, which change and shape our physical world.

'These decisions are made on the basis of a complex experience of sensual and intellectual perception, of memory and association, filtered through a cultural apparatus of which we remain largely unaware,' the exhibition explained.

'It would be easy to make the fashionable case against technology or the developers. Technology in building and elsewhere has made us comfortable enough to worry about the meal after next, a luxury denied to previous cultures.

'Developers are prime movers, takers of risks, rewarded with titles and followed like racehorses by the gamblers on the Stock Exchange. They play the environment game for high stakes, and have been known

When you are looking for a solution to what you are told is an architectural problem – remember, it may not be a building.
RON HERRON
Contemporary Architects (1980)

occasionally to lose their shirts.

'Our future lies . . . above all in our own involvement. We should not wait for the motorway to arrive at the front door before raising a protest.

'There is a mechanism within the law which allows everyone to be involved in environmental decisions. But all laws require exercise. They have to be used, and explored in mutual confrontations. A society which accepts the working of its bureaucracy without protest deserves to be strangled with red tape.'

Since those words were written in 1973, protest and public participation have grown on a scale which would never have been dreamed of then. Attitudes to many controversial issues have sharpened: urban motorways; high-rise housing; anonymous speculative office blocks; needless destruction of old but beautiful buildings and historic town centres; and central and local government paternalism. People are much more prepared to stand up and be counted and more likely to get their own way.

Edward Cullinan
Partner, Edward Cullinan Architects, London

The architect must produce something which is visually beautiful as well as socially useful.
HRH THE PRINCE OF WALES
addressing architects at
Hampton Court Palace (1984)

Edward Cullinan was as surprised as everyone else when the Prince of Wales identified him as 'a man after my own heart' in his controversial speech at Hampton Court Palace in 1984, when the Royal Institute of British Architects celebrated its 150th anniversary.

What prompted this remark was that the Prince shared Cullinan's belief that 'the architect must produce something that is visually beautiful as well as socially useful'. Most people might think this should be taken for granted; in fact it says a lot about Edward Cullinan's approach to architecture, which he defines as 'a celebration of necessity'.

Cullinan's designs and working drawings were the subject of an exhibition at the Heinz Gallery, London, in 1984. The exhibits included details of many private houses, local authority housing, the Minster Lovell study centre, offices and training colleges for British Olivetti, and several community centres and buildings for the handicapped. His practice was one of four firms short-listed for the extension to the Royal Opera House, Covent Garden.

Cullinan took a first-class degree at Cambridge and a diploma from the Architectural Association in London. Then he went to California and met Frank Lloyd Wright, whom in many ways he emulates in his commitment to a democratic architecture and his conviction that the ego is the key to creativity and innovation.

But he is also an architect in the tradition of the master builder. His principal hobby is building, and he is as comfortable with a hammer in his hands as with a 4B pencil. He has built four houses.

St Mary's Church, Barnes, as rebuilt by Edward Cullinan.

Edward Cullinan Architects, the small co-operative practice in north London which he founded in 1959, pursues a middle course between such Hi-Tech architects as Norman Foster and Richard Rogers on the one hand and Classical Revivalists and Post-Modernists such as Quinlan Terry and Terry Farrell on the other. Architectural historians maintain that he is a direct heir to a tradition which can be traced through the Arts and Crafts movement to Pugin a century and a half ago.

'I am happy for historians to connect me by umbilical cord to the past, but I am much more aware of being taught by Peter Smithson, working for Sir Denys Lasdun, and therefore being greatly influenced by Berthold Lubetkin.' Lubetkin, with his firm Tecton, put English modern architecture on the world map with the Penguin pool at London Zoo and the Highpoint flats of the 1930s.

His professional peers enjoy the way he creates places for activity and the skill with which materials are used, while the public enjoys the picturesque qualities of his work. He believes that an observer should

Edward Cullinan. Architecture is, he says, 'a celebration of necessity'.

The problem of architecture as I see it is the problem of all art – the elimination of the human element from the consideration of form.
Professor-Architect Otto Friedrich Silenus in
Decline and Fall
by EVELYN WAUGH

be able to see and comprehend how a building is made. That is essential to its enjoyment. The choices the designer makes should be evident. Cullinan invites discussion and criticism of his work from those for whom he builds, to try to make his architecture more responsive to need. In rebuilding the Church of St Mary at Barnes, which had been burnt down in 1978, those extra 'clients' numbered around 300.

Like his buildings, he is both a romantic (defined by Frank Lloyd Wright as 'wanting things to be better than they are') and an optimist (in believing they actually will get better). He hopes that the Prince's comments at Hampton Court will lead to a more rigorous discussion of architecture, and eventually raise the public's visual abilities to the same level as its appreciation of literature and music.

Jeremy Dixon
Partner, Jeremy Dixon, London

Jeremy Dixon set up his own practice in 1977 after working with Alison and Peter Smithson and the Milton Keynes Development Corporation. He also has a joint practice with Building Design Partnership to design the £55-million extension to the Royal Opera House, Covent Garden. His best-known work to date is a housing scheme at St Mark's Road, North Kensington, London.

Housing at St Mark's Road, North Kensington, by Jeremy Dixon, picks up visual references from the surrounding streets and re-interprets them in a modern idiom.

'The front façade uses elements extracted from the surrounding streets – porches, bay windows, stairs, gateposts – exploiting particularly features at right angles to the façade, in order to produce in perspective the rhythms associated with a street. Each house has a front door to the street, a garden and a rear elevation distinct and different from the front façade. The scheme attempted to demonstrate that it is possible to maintain a sympathetic relationship with the existing fabric of the area, and at the same time to keep the strength of geometrical composition and form necessary to the integrity of a new building that does not apologise for its existence.'

Dixon's approach is contextual in picking up local references and re-interpreting them in a modern idiom, an important development away from the strictures of the Modern Movement.

Sir Philip Dowson
Partner, Arup Associates, London

Sir Philip Dowson is an architect who thinks like a master builder or an engineer: he does not talk about designing buildings so much as making them, and that is something his practice, Arup Associates, does extremely well. In addition to winning a string of awards for such buildings as the Maltings Concert Hall at Snape, the John Player factory at Nottingham, IBM at Havant, the Central Electricity Generating Board offices at Bristol, and Wiggins Teape (paper makers) offices at Basingstoke, he has also received his profession's highest accolade: the Royal Gold Medal for Architecture in 1981.

He switched from training as an engineer to training as an architect after the War, and was offered a job on a short contract by consulting engineers Ove Arup & Partners in 1953. He stayed on, and in 1963 the decision was taken to form a new partnership of architects and engineers called Arup Associates.

The interior of the Finsbury Square office development, London, by Arup Associates.

Seven different professions work together at Arup Associates, about 110 people in total, divided into teams of 15 to 25 on particular projects. The Associates have worked on the Liverpool Garden Festival building, planned to convert to a sports hall when the festival ended; new BBC Radio headquarters in Edinburgh; feasibility studies for the London Docklands light railway; alterations and additions to the Imperial War Museum; and designs for a new sports and recreation facility for the diplomatic quarter of Riyadh, Saudi Arabia.

But unlike some practices, Arup Associates use technology as a means to an end, not as an end to be glorified in its own right. It is part of the search for what Sir Philip Dowson calls 'a new architecture of humanism'.

Terry Farrell
Senior Partner, Terry Farrell Partnership, London

Terry Farrell's conversion of a car repair workshop into the headquarters of TV-am has confirmed him as Britain's leading Post-Modern architect, comparable to America's Michael Graves. It was a highly successful example of instant image-making architecture. 'It is very serious architecture,' says Farrell, when challenged with the accusation that his work has more in common with Mickey Mouse then Michelangelo. 'It has colour and ornament, it meets human aesthetic needs in a free-style combining many different elements, a collage of images and forms.'

It would be wrong not to take Farrell seriously, for his Post-Modernism is only one facet of his pragmatic approach to architecture. He produced an alternative plan for the Mansion House site in the City, for SAVE Britain's Heritage (which rehabilitated most of the existing Victorian buildings due for demolition if the Mies van der Rohe office block had gone ahead); and he can revert to other, more appropriate imagery for other types of buildings – for example, the headquarters of the Thames Water Authority, the exhibition gallery at Alexandra Palace, and two large bank office developments in the City of London which he is currently working on. Like the Docklands conversion of a shed into television studios, he is probably happiest when producing a decorated Hi-Tech style, or Dec-Tech as he calls it. His new headquarters for Henley Royal Regatta is a cross between a classical temple and a Victorian boathouse.

In a monograph of his work published in 1984, Farrell concluded an essay on 'British Architecture After Modernism' thus: "The real lessons for British architects from American Post-Modern Classicism is that the British are too precious and over-stuffy in their concerns. If British Modernism's failure was that it took itself too earnestly, too joylessly and seriously, it seems inevitable that establishment modern architects prefer Quinlan Terry's 'properly done' Classicism to anything freewheeling and interpretive like Venturi, Stern or Graves".

Terry Farrell, Britain's leading Post-Modernist and advocate of Dec-Tech.

Sight is one of man's great gifts. To have eyes that do not see but merely record, is to be dead to at least one aspect of the world. Whether architecture is to deteriorate into a crude commercialism, whether it is to be devitalized by subservience to architectural clichés, *or whether it is to become one of the finest means of expression of mankind, will largely depend on a new visual awareness. Wtihout this, architecture is but music to the deaf.*
RALPH TUBBS
The Englishman Builds (1945)

Norman Foster

Partner, Foster Associates, London

Above: Norman Foster, Royal Gold Medallist for Architecture in 1983.

Right: The Renault Centre, Swindon, by Norman Foster.

An architect requires a great many men to erect his building. But he does not ask them to vote on his design. They work together by free agreement and each is free in his proper function. An architect uses steel, glass, concrete produced by others. But the materials remain just so much steel, glass and concrete until he touches them.

HOWARD ROARK

the architect as 'hero and genius' in Ayn Rand's *The Fountainhead* (1947)

Norman Foster shares with Richard Rogers, with whom he used to be in partnership, an approach to architecture which creates places for human activity within carefully crafted buildings. Although the architecture is often visually stunning and therefore photogenic, the research and attitude to each project in fact creates the design solution.

'Architecture has to be a fusion between something that works in terms of real needs and at the level of the spirit. It has to produce spaces which make you feel good, comfortable, good places to be whether inside or out,' Foster says. 'That tradition was very powerful in the nineteenth-century, but I now fear we are witnessing a polarisation where one type of building is regarded as "functional, profitable and speculative" and has all the bad overtones, and others are regarded as "special, precious, expensive, high culture and therefore good architecture". That is very worrying because the best buildings of any age have truly integrated needs and have been sympathetic and sensitive to

social aspects. Buildings are about the public as well as the private domain.'

Shared idealism and endeavour go a long way to producing the right results in human terms, and quality cannot be measured only in money terms: often the best solution costs no more than the worst. His practice can spend months talking at length to people before starting work on the design process.

In the Sainsbury Centre for the Visual Arts in Norwich a number of separate functions were combined which would normally have been housed in different buildings. Gallery space, research facilities, a restaurant and museum storage were brought together to provide a 'richer mix'.

At the Willis Faber headquarters in Ipswich, a large office building was cleverly designed with curving glass walls sympathetically following the medieval street pattern. The building is 'open plan', but Foster chose to convey people from floor to floor by 'enjoyable escalators' rather than 'boxed-in lifts'.

Some of these ideas were also used in the Hongkong and Shanghai Banking Corporation headquarters, opened in Hong Kong in 1985. The nature of the high-rise building was thought through again from first principles. The potentially intimidating scale of the building was broken down into a series of smaller spaces which Foster compares with villages on top of each other. The need for flexible planning influenced the way floors are suspended from the gigantic masts; that the building can grow over time. The floor area can be increased by about 30 per cent without changing the structure. Aircraft floor construction was used to ease the runs of services. Also, large floor panels are so light that two people can move then around quite easily.

Increasing public awareness of architecture gives him optimism for the future, because it will help to raise standards. 'There is an awakening of the public conscience and the public are leading the media in the debate. I see that as very positive, very progressive and far more relevant to standards of architecture than consenting critics holding private conversations.'

The best way to improve standards in architecture is to complain, he believes, as one would about food or any other service. 'Take an active interest; be discriminating. Criticism actually sharpens performance if it is constructive. If you are interested in better architecture, then campaign for better architecture.'

He received the Royal Gold Medal for Architecture in 1983.

Barry Gasson
Partner, Barry Gasson Architect, Glasgow

Barry Gasson trained at Birmingham School of Architecture, followed by a graduate degree course at Columbia University in America. Afterwards he worked in Philip Johnson's office in New York, returning in the later 1960s to teach at Cambridge (he also taught in Dublin, in California, and at the Mackintosh school in Glasgow) and to take part in a number of architectural competitions.

Along with 250 others he entered the competition to design a new museum for Glasgow's Burrell Collection in 1972, and he won.

The building is a triumph. It combines art and nature in its parkland

A more expressive technology is very much part of an architecture which follows on after modernism . . . The European tradition, particularly of Arts and Crafts and Art Nouveau, took so much of its inspiration from how things were made; the studded wall-cladding of Otto Wagner, the elaborate but prefabricated cast-iron elements of Hector Guimard's metro stations and the sculptured r.s.j's of C. R. Mackintosh were all outstanding combinations of art and technology.

TERRY FARRELL
'British Architecture After Modernism' in *Terry Farrell*
Architectural Monographs (1984)

[Architecture] is an art purely of invention – and invention is the most painful and most difficult exercise of the human mind.

SIR JOHN SOANE

The Burrell Collection Building, Glasgow, by Barry Gasson. The glass walls integrate the building into the surrounding landscape.

setting just outside Glasgow city centre. 'It is a magical collection,' says Gasson, 'full of allure and fascination. I wanted to bring light into the building, the changing light of the days and the seasons, and the surrounding woodlands, so that the landscaping becomes part of the architecture.'

The £17-million museum opened in October 1984 to great critical acclaim. In the first six months it had 500,000 visitors.

Piers Gough

Partner, Campbell, Zogolovitch, Wilkinson & Gough, London

The duty of the artist is to strain against the bounds of the existing style . . . and only this procedure makes the development of architecture possible.
PHILIP JOHNSON
in *Conversations with Artists*
by Selden Rodman

Piers Gough formed a partnership with Roger Zogolovitch and Rex Wilkinson while a student at the Architectural Association in London in 1968. Three years later, they went their separate ways, but they re-united in 1975, when Nick Campbell joined them. Since then they have built up a practice which specialises in converting existing buildings to new uses and in speculative housing with a fresh, populist approach and a good deal of wit.

'Modern architecture is elitist; it always has been,' says Gough, 'even if its intention originally was socialist. The most difficult thing is to design buildings which people like to look at – architects are out of practice as there is no ready vocabulary of delight except developers' Georgian.'

His response is to borrow styles and forms from any previous historical source to create deliberate, populist imagery. Very often this imagery includes 'seductive curves' which were virtually banished by the Modern Movement. Gough designed the exhibition of the work of architect Sir Edwin Lutyens at the Hayward Gallery, London in 1981. 'The lesson it taught me was that great architecture could be made out of very ordinary, vernacular building materials and styles. Architects can create something wonderful without resorting to "architectural details". But bad architects should stick to classical design,' he says.

Most of CZWG's commissions have been in London, with developments in Hackney, Mile End, the King's Road, and at China Wharf, Wapping, refurbishing Thameside flats. Some years ago they won an ideas competition with a £3-million plan to build a roller-coaster on Newcastle's Quayside. The 80 ft-high structure would have been built at a Tyneside shipyard and floated up-river. Lights along the half-mile structure would have spelt out 'Newcastle', providing an instant image for the city comparable (it was hoped) to the Eiffel Tower in Paris or the Statue of Liberty in New York.

Bruce Graham
Partner, Skidmore, Owings & Merrill, Chicago

Bruce Graham, leader of the design team of one of the largest multi-disciplinary practices in America, is responsible for two of the world's highest buildings – the John Hancock Center and the Sears Tower, both in Chicago. In the John Hancock Center diagonal trusses are expressed on the outside of the building, an attempt to relate the size of the building to the people outside it. 'When I first looked at very tall buildings as a young architect,' says Graham, 'I was impressed with the fact that there was no sense of scale to buildings and what was missing was structure. If you look at the tradition of architecture, it's structure that gives architecture scale.'

The Sears Tower (1450 ft, 110 stories) is the highest building in the world. The structure is made up of nine tubes, each 75 ft square but of varying height, bundled together to give added wind resistance. 'Tall buildings,' Graham says, 'exist comfortably in some places and not in others. For example, they're not comfortable in Cairo or London and other European cities. But there's a fitness to tall buildings in Chicago that doesn't exist in many other places.'

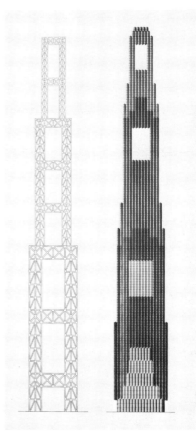

SOM's design for what would be the tallest building in the world if it were built: the Chicago World Trade Center.

Opposite: Hongkong and Shanghai Bank. The £500-million headquarters of the Hongkong and Shanghai Banking Corporation, in Hong Kong, was completed in 1985. Designed by Norman Foster, it is among the world's most sophisticated new buildings. A steel cathedral for the high priests of banking, the prefabricated kit of parts from eighty countries was assembled on site in just over four years. Floors are hung from eight steel masts, allowing clear spans of 100 ft; and there is a 170 ft high atrium banking hall at its base.

Right: Bruce Graham's Sears Tower, the world's tallest building (right) with Helmut Jahn's One, South Wacker Building, Chicago.

Opposite top left: Arcosanti. Inspired by Frank Lloyd Wright and Antonio Gaudí, the Italian visionary Paolo Soleri has been building Arcosanti in the Arizona desert since 1970. It is based on his philosophy of 'arcology', i.e. 'architecture' + 'ecology'. It is being built by largely student labour, who live a monastic lifestyle.

Opposite top right: Byker Wall. Community architect Ralph Erskine had his office in a former funeral parlour on the site of the huge Byker housing redevelopment in Newcastle. The scale of the building is broken down by the use of colourful, patterned brickwork and timber balconies. It even won an award for the 'Best Kept Village in Britain'.

Opposite bottom: Headquarters, Thames Water. British architect Terry Farrell's offices and Water Treatment Centre at Reading combines decoration and Hi-Tech, which he calls Dec-Tech. The Thames Water Authority's logo, of gently rising and falling waves, is alluded to in the bench seating, glazing and colour scheme.

Dr Rod Hackney
Managing Director, Rod Hackney & Associates, Macclesfield

'Community architecture' was a term coined in 1975 to describe Rod Hackney's work with a group of tenants and owner-occupiers in Macclesfield. He organised the people to fight off the threat of demolition of their homes, then helped them repair the properties. Hackney's work was perhaps the first example of significant change in the professional's

THE BANDWAGON ROLLS...

Community architect Rod Hackney leading the movement's 'bandwagon', with some help from the Prince of Wales, by Louis Hellman in the *Architects' Journal.*

role. As discussed in 'New Directions', the architect had become an 'enabler' helping people to sort out their own problems rather than imposing his own solution.

The community architecture movement has mushroomed since then. There are perhaps 1,000 architects now doing this type of work. And Hackney's workload has followed: he now has 11 offices from Stirling to Leicester, each one located in the street where his clients live. His total staff is now about 70, including 13 from the Manpower Services Commission scheme.

Work includes a £1-million project for rehabilition of older homes and self-build new homes in Stirling; industrial regeneration projects in Chesterfield and Burnley (where he is landowner, project manager, developer and architect); and a partly self-build scheme of 32 new homes in a development valued at more than £1 million, called Roan Court, also in Macclesfield, where he is also builder of some of the houses and estate agent.

His move into development – which has only recently been allowed under the RIBA's code of professional conduct – is an important one for Hackney. It is a matter of survival. 'Half my architectural practice is community-based, half the normal type of general practice. But there is a need to subsidise the community work, and the only way this can be done is by making a profit on building, on developing, and on the design/ contract administration side as well.'

Hackney, considered a rebel by the RIBA when he started as a community activist, eventually became a member of its ruling council. He was one of the few architects on it not concerned about numbers entering the profession: 'Architects are working for new clients – just as doctors did when the National Health Service started, and solicitors did with the introduction of Legal Aid. The new code relaxations allow

After consulting all the pundits, however exalted or however humble, architects will not be able to evade their responsibility to create an architecture that evokes the promise, and so provokes the action, for a more sane society to come. Only then are they more likely to receive the confidence and respect of the public community they so assiduously seek.

BERTHOLD LUBETKIN
RIBA President's invitation lecture (1985)

architects to expand their activities, especially in the areas where they are most needed – the inner cities. There they can make a very positive contribution by harnessing the massive human resource in transforming a decaying environment.'

He is architectural adviser to the Prince of Wales.

Helmut Jahn
Partner, Murphy, Jahn, Chicago

Jahn came to America in 1966, at the age of 26, from West Germany. He designs monumental buildings which blend a Mannerist glorification of technology with a decorative, contextual art. Structure and services are expressed with honesty, yet in their external appearance his buildings take on the mantle of their urban surroundings. 'In America,

The State of Illinois Center, Chicago, by Helmut Jahn.

Hi-Tech is not treated as an end in itself,' he says. His architecture is closer to the work of James Stirling rather than that of Norman Foster or Richard Rogers.

His most recent completed building is the State of Illinois Center in Chicago, a glass-and-steel rotunda with an inclined roof enclosing a huge public lobby at the centre of what is otherwise a private federal government building. The interior resembles a NASA space shuttle launching-pad, and he makes innovative use of structure and servicing, such as the photo-electric cells which control the lighting level in the lobby.

Jahn is best known for his 'designer architecture', particularly sky-scapers across America and in South Africa. Two of the most interesting projects are in New York: Park Avenue Tower at 65 East 55th Street, opposite the AT & T and IBM towers; and 42 Lexington Avenue, near the Chrysler Building.

The Park Avenue scheme is in the early twentieth-century New York 'setback' style, a granite and glass obelisk with a tapering shaft rising 36 storeys, crowned by an open four-sided pyramid. At Lexington Avenue the architect is building a column which relates back to the Chicago Tribune Tower competition entry by Adolf Loos in 1922. The 23-storey tower has a base, a shaft, and a capital which flares out at the top at the same height as the Chrysler steps inwards.

Eva Jiricna, London

Eva Jiricna came to London in 1969 to work for the GLC Architects' Department in their schools division for a year. The Russian invasion prevented her from going back to Czechoslovakia.

She trained as an architect–engineer in Prague but took the RIBA's Part III final exams in Britain. She was then the job architect on the Brighton Marina project with the Louis de Soissons Partnership. She worked on the interiors of the new £157-million Lloyd's headquarters building in the City of London for Richard Rogers, but her plans were not executed. She likes using hard, bright and tough industrial materials in her designs for shops in London (for Joseph in South Molton Street, Le Caprice, Kenzo) and flats for friends.

She has a flair for design competitions – of which she has won several: the Westminster Pier competition by the GLC, and the Dunlopillo Home for the year 2000 among them. 'I like competitions because they test how far you can go, you create your own brief and limitations and can give rein to your imagination – there is no-one else to blame and the design is not compromised by others.'

The practice of architecture is becoming more and more complex, she believes, as the profession is now only responsible for one part of the whole building process. The organisational aspects of building – and how well the issues have been understood – create or destroy good architecture, and that includes the aesthetics of design.

There still remains the architect's role to be assessed in connection with the urban nightmare. Despite an uninterrupted record of bungled cities, Americans have preserved a touching faith in the practitioners of architecture. This faith, unshaken by experience, is no doubt a residue from the time when architects were the prodigies of the human race, combining in one person the talents and skills of sculptor, painter and writer. (Le Corbusier was the last of this tribe of complete artists.) Perhaps also the transferred uses of the word architect – as the spiritual parent of a scheme – brought a certain loftiness to it. Not that architects ever ranked among national heroes. Far from it. They are one of the least conspicuous professional groups. Artists' and writers' names may become household words, but not architects'. Architects rarely make headlines, and then only in the Sunday supplements of metropolitan newspapers.
BERNARD RUDOFSKY
Streets for People:
A Primer for Americans (1969)

Czech-born Eva Jiricna: design flair.

Philip Johnson
Partner, Johnson, Burgee, New York

Philip Johnson, who coined the term 'International Style', worked with Mies van der Rohe on the Seagram Building, then designed the Post-Modern AT&T Building for Manhattan.

Architect, *n. One who drafts a plan of your house, and plans a draft of your money.*
AMBROSE BIERCE (1881–1911)
The Devil's Dictionary

Philip Johnson is full of surprises. In 1932, with Henry-Russell Hitchcock, he coined the term 'International Style', which became synonymous with the Modern Movement for the next fifty years. He was instrumental in bringing Ludwig Mies van der Rohe to America in 1937, and worked with him on the Seagram Building in New York, where he still has his office. But in 1978 he produced his designs for the new headquarters of the American Telephone & Telegraph Company (AT&T) the world's tallest Chippendale highboy.

Ada Louise Huxtable, New York's leading architecture critic, described the 650-ft-high rose-grey granite hulk as a 'monumental leg-pull'. But then Johnson, 80 in 1986, has been pulling other people's legs – usually members of his profession – for as long as anyone can remember.

From being Mies's greatest admirer and propagandist, he has become his greatest critic. The International Style, he says, was just another period of architecture whose time has now passed. 'It succeeded because it was cheaper for developers than Edwardian. It became developers' architecture, as well represented in the work of Colonel Seifert,' he says mischievously. For him, like many others, Mies's maxim, 'Less is more' has been superseded by Robert Venturi's 'Less is a bore'. When he taught at Yale twenty years ago he scrawled on the blackboard 'You cannot not know history'.

Today Johnson borrows from any style he considers appropriate for a particular commission. 'We do not believe in anything today. Anyway, belief is not necessary for beauty.' His Pittsburgh Plate Glass Company building is a Gothic fantasy, while his 42nd Street development in New York was described in *Harper's* as the 'architecture of salon painting'. The glass box will never be the same again, and it was the AT&T building which did it. Crenellated castles and French Empire style also provide inspiration for this self-confessed plagiarist. But then Johnson said, once he had attained the age of 70, that he was no longer bothered by what other people thought. A Chicago architect recently described his work as 'beyond morality', to which he replied, 'I would work for the devil himself.'

Charles Jencks wrote of the architect in 1973: 'This honest amorality is exactly what gives [him] his integrity. He, more than any other architect, has been true to fashion, an affluent society and city life.' His architecture is Republican, monumental and corporate, packaged in the same way as any Madison Avenue campaign to sell soap, candy bars, or soft drinks – another product of the American consumer's dream.

What epitaph would he choose for himself? 'Philip Johnson was not America's greatest architect, but he was its most influential.'

John Portman
Principal, John Portman & Associates, Atlanta

As the first of a new breed of architects-turned-developers, John Portman was called before the ethics committee of the American Institute of Architects in 1965 to explain the possible conflict of interest. He satisfied it that there was none, and since then many other architects in America, Britain and elsewhere have followed his lead. To him, architecture is still first an art, then secondly business. He runs his architectural and engineering practice as well as being chief executive of Portman Properties and chairman of the Atlanta Merchandise Mart.

He is the creator of some of the most spatially extravagant buildings of the twentieth century, notably the Hyatt Regency Hotel in San Francisco, used for some of the interior scenes of the disaster movie, *Towering Inferno*. It is an astonishing building with a 22-storey atrium lobby, filled with fountains, cafés, birds in a three-storey aviary, sculpture, and a cocktail lounge whose 14-ton roof hangs from a single cable. All this is too much for some of his critics, particularly other architects. His work was once compared to Disneyland, to which his response was: 'I plead guilty'.

In *The Architect as Developer*, written with Jonathan Barnett, Portman urged architects to acquire a financial nose so that they could become 'master co-ordinators for the physical development of entire cities'. Buildings could be more attractive – and show a larger financial return – if their designers also wove 'elements of sensory appeal' into them. At the same time, it must be said, many of his buildings are introverted to the extent that they turn their back on the rest of the city.

Still, he believes and practises architecture as the most public art, experiential as well as simply visual, by ensuring the senses are stimulated as one moves through his buildings. The trouble with so much modern architecture, he says, is that some of the needs of the people it was designed for simply got left out.

The architectural horrors with which the public is often confronted are not merely due to the incompetence of architects, but to the crumbling civilisation in which we live. After all, what is the visual equivalent of a world that allows 40,000 children to die needlessly each day, while the United States of America alone spends $26 million an hour on armaments?

BERTHOLD LUBETKIN
RIBA President's invitation lecture (1985)

Richard Rogers
Partner, Richard Rogers & Partners, London

Richard Rogers, who received the Royal Gold Medal for Architecture in 1985, was born of British parents in Florence, and studied in London and at Yale University, where another British architect, James Stirling, was a tutor. Later he was in practice with Norman and Wendy Foster and Su Rogers in Team 4, 1963–8. His energy and enthusiasm have an overlay of international experience which comes through his approach to architecture as a social art.

He believes that architecture is a response to the environment and

Richard Rogers, Royal Gold Medallist for Architecture in 1985.

circumstances which give birth to it, and that includes the planning system, the attitude of groups such as the Royal Fine Art Commission and the conservation lobby, media coverage and public opinion. 'Architecture is an outcome of the social revolution that we have had since 1850 – it arrived as a result of the Industrial Revolution – because no-one works in isolation any more. Humanity works together and we are all influenced by each other.'

All periods of architecture, he believes, are to some extent revolutionary, so the sometimes startling innovations and appearance of new buildings need time to be assimilated and to become familiar. Many of the problems associated with modern architecture are really those of the way it has been used, not something intrinsic in its principles.

'But architecture is becoming much more conscious of the relation of cities to history, of what history has to tell us about the way cities are built.' The way cities work, how people use them, and the need for flexibility to allow for changes in use and function, are issues which are constantly raised in Rogers' architecture, whether the buildings are primarily for public use or for private use.

The Pompidou Centre at Beaubourg in Paris, which he designed with Renzo Piano, is his most famous building. On the question as to whether it is a French building, he replies that the street life which goes on around it 'absorbs the building and in the end makes it French'. Although it stands for the centralistion of culture – in a way which is alien in Britian though not in America – it is probably the most accessible and inviting building of its type.

The success of the centre he puts down to its over-lapping activities. 'We actually set up a "non-programme activities team" which searched for activities which would draw people of all ages, all colours, all creeds. The whole idea was to encourage a culture for all and not purely for those who happen to have a specific type of education, which is the problem we have here in Britain. The South Bank in London is highly élite, it serves a cultural élite, and I am very much against that idea – or of buildings which only serve an élite.'

It is significant that the architect should consider it part of his role to ensure that the building was fully used.

Rogers chooses to clothe his social art in a Hi-Tech skin which gives it its imagery, sometimes called 'oil refinery architecture' or, in the case of Pompidou, likened to a cultural supermarket. But for him such aesthetic preoccupations are secondary to the aim of encouraging social interaction. That is why, he believes, the Pompidou Centre attracts more visitors each year than the Louvre and Eiffel Tower combined – more even than Disneyland.

He thinks the South Bank should be linked with the rest of the capital and should combine a mixture of uses. He has investigated providing both in his proposals, now abandoned, for Coin Street. An airport-type moving pavement across one of the Thames bridges could link Trafalgar Square, Leicester Square and Piccadilly Circus with the area south of the river; or buildings could be built on bridges like the Ponte Vecchio in Florence.

Flexibility is built into all Rogers' buildings. At the new Lloyd's headquarters building in the City of London, by providing large floor areas uncluttered by structural columns or service ducts, small cells or larger areas can be used for a variety of functions. Lloyd's had already occupied four buildings this century, so the brief was to create a space flexible enough to accommodate expansion. Information technology was more or less invented during the time it took to design and erect the building completed in 1986.

Shops, restaurants and other public facilities are located at street level, a conscious attempt to relate the public to what is primarily a private institution.

Keith Scott
Chairman, Building Design Partnership, Preston

The Ealing Centre in west London, formally opened by the Queen in 1985, was voted one of the best modern buildings in the capital by viewers of *Thames News*, the regional television news programme, a year before it was even completed. Top came Hillingdon Civic Centre, also in west London, designed by Robert Matthew, Johnson-Marshall & Partners, led by Andrew Derbyshire.

Both are examples of building in a new vernacular of bricks and tiles on pitched roofs, more informal layout, consciously picturesque features, and decoration. The Ealing Centre, built in the 'Queen of the

The £157-million Lloyd's of London, Hi-Tech post-Pompidou.

The Ealing Centre, west London, by Keith Scott of Building Design Partnership, voted one the best modern buildings in the capital by viewers of *Thames News*.

Isaiah Berlin once commented that people could be characterised as hedgehogs or foxes. There were those with a fixed single strategy and those who survived by continuous adaptation. Since the decline in influence of doctrinaire modernism (and the rigid stances of the other 'isms' of the early part of the twentieth-century) it has become more and more a time for foxes. Today to establish a growth and continuity in one's personal work means responding to an ever-widening theatre of influences within an overall climate of rapid change. Progress inevitably involves the ebbing and flowing of response to these stimuli; shifting patterns emerge, come into focus, blur, fade and then return.

TERRY FARRELL

'Hedgehogs and Foxes' in
Terry Farrell
Architectural Monographs (1984)

Suburbs', could almost be a medieval fortress, with its towers and turrets as well as more obviously Edwardian bay windows and gables. But the popularity of the scheme is undeniable.

Keith Scott, the BDP partner in charge, says: 'The architecture reflects the spirit of the age we are living in now, not outdated Modernist dogma. Some architects call it "Noddy architecture" but it is done with sincerity and has a credibility and acceptability with local people.'

In fact the original comprehensive redevelopment plan of 1968 for a 15-acre site in the centre of the suburb, called for a 17-storey office block, 10-storey blocks of flats and two multi-storey car parks following a pattern we had come to expect. One thousand homes were also to be demolished. Residents protested, however, and they won a campaign under the slogan 'Put the heart back into Ealing,' which resulted in a public inquiry in 1976.

After the victory, local residents were involved in the process of interviewing rival developers and their architects. Joy Anthony and Corinne Templer represented local people and described the experience to the *Sunday Times Magazine*:

'We felt that after all the work we had done we must have something worth looking at – a town centre, not a sterile lump of concrete. It must have life in it. Ealing had been an important suburb; it had its own character, and we wanted that to be maintained, enhanced and reflected.'

'The brief made it absolutely clear that the public of Ealing were looking for a design which reflected the past and paid homage to what they saw as the "Spirit of Ealing",' says Scott. 'In 1979 the architectural profession was at the beginning of a reaction and was reappraising its design assumptions. It was obvious that the public had given a firm thumbs-down to the mainstream architectural direction since the Second World War.

'They were tired of glass boxes and they hated concrete. Architects of my generation had fundamentally to reappraise our whole training, in which we were taught that "Form should follow Function", that "Houses are Machines for Living In", and that "Ornament is a Crime". We therefore looked backwards through historical record to see why the architecture of the past *had* been acceptable to public taste.

'As a result of this study some architects have completely misunderstood the purpose of this "vernacular" movement. They seem to think that one can stick on to buildings bits of historical detail regardless of context. For me this is not architecture because it has no inherent sincerity. In my view much Post-Modern architecture is simply wallpaper and has no more relevance to the art of architecture than muzak has to Beethoven.'

Colin Stansfield Smith
Hampshire County Architect, Winchester

In his 40th year Colin Stansfield Smith made the unusual move from private practice into the public sector. 'Architecture is popular in Hampshire,' he maintains, by which he means the sort of modern architecture which he is responsible for, produced by his own department of 180 (of which 40 are architects and architectural technicians) or put out to Portsmouth and Southampton city architects and private firms.

The emphasis is on design, 'put the art back into architecture', which has resulted in a large crop of awards in recent years. The work produced by Hampshire county architects has been described as 'gothic' and 'picturesque'; it replaces the standardised system building which characterised the architecture before Stansfield Smith's arrival.

'We are trying to redress the balance in favour of individual buildings,' he says. 'Social architecture does not attract the same interest as it used to in recent years; it had become almost a set of procedures, but we are trying to get away from stultifying and stereotype buildings.'

The brevity of human life gives a melancholy to the profession of the architect.
RALPH WALDO EMERSON
Journals (1842)

The demand that all buildings should become works of architecture . . . is strictly offensive to common sense . . . One might possibly stipulate that architecture is a social institution related to building in much the same way that literature is to speech.
COLIN ROWE
Collage City (1978)

Yateley Newlands School, Hampshire. 'Social architecture' is still in vogue in Hampshire County architects' department.

Red House Health Centre, Eastleigh, Hampshire, designed by architects in Colin Stansfield Smith's local authority department.

James Stirling, Royal Gold Medallist for Architecture in 1980.

James Stirling

Partner, James Stirling, Michael Wilford Associates, London

It was American architectural historian, Charles Jencks, who said that 'Big Jim' Stirling was Britain's best architect since Nicholas Hawksmoor. Probably few architects, at least, would disagree that he is among the country's top three living architects, the other two – Norman Foster and Richard Rogers – were both post-graduate students of his at Yale in the early 1960s.

Certainly Stirling's early buildings, such as the Leicester University engineering building and the History Faculty at Cambridge, with their Hi-Tech imagery, were among the most potent and influential creations of the post-war generation of architects, even though both have experienced constructional problems. He received the Royal Gold Medal for Architecture in 1980.

But by 1985, Stirling reported that he had moved on and entered a different phase. 'The Modern Movement has run out of steam,' he says. 'We have entered a new period of evolution where there are no absolutes, rather a combination of Hi-Tech with traditional elements and memories of past.'

Interior and exterior of Stirling's spectacular but problematic History Faculty Library, Cambridge.

Architects never felt the urge to establish ethical precepts for the performance of their profession, as did the medical fraternity. No equivalent of the Hippocratic oath exists for them. Hippocrates' promise that 'the regimen I adopt shall be for the benefit of my patients according to my ability and judgement, and not for their hurt or for any wrong' has no counterpart in their book. Criticism within the profession – the only conceivable way to spread a sense of responsibility among its members – is tabooed by their own codified standards of practice. To bolster their own ego, architects hold their own beauty contests, award each other prizes, decorate each other with gold medals, and make light of the damning fact that they do not amount to any moral force in this country. The situation is not altogether new. 'No profession has done its duty until it has furnished a victim,' said Disraeli; '. . . suppose an architect were hanged. Terror has its aspiration, as well as competition.'
BERNARD RUDOFSKY
Streets for People:
A Primer for Americans (1969)

His arts centre for Stuttgart, opened in 1984, illustrates what he meant. It is a landmark building, full of references to other buildings in the city and to its immediate context. It was his first major building for ten years, and virtually all the work of this period – except the new Clore Gallery extension to the Tate in London – has been for sites outside Britain.

Stirling decries the Post-Modern work of Michael Graves in the US and Terry Farrell in Britain because it has rejected architecture immediately preceding it. He supports Quinlan Terry's Classicism 'where it is justified – it's sad there aren't more architects like him', but he backed the proposed Mies van der Rohe office tower for the City of London, as he believes the capital needs an outstanding example of modern architecture. When the scheme was turned down by the Government in

You come over here [i.e. to Britain] and you find the best modern architecture in the world.
PHILIP JOHNSON
American architect

All sensible and sensitive people know that modern architecture is bad and horrible.
PAUL JOHNSON
British writer

1985, Stirling was appointed as Mies' successor by the client, Peter Palumbo.

Britain's 'best living architect' is also one of its greatest enigmas.

Quinlan Terry
Partner, Erith & Terry, Dedham, near Colchester

Quinlan Terry, unofficial leader of the Classical Revivalists.

'I long to see a genuine Classical revival in this country,' says Quinlan Terry.

He joined Raymond Erith in 1962. Together they worked in the classical tradition on Kings Walden Bury, a Georgian-style country house built in 1968; the Gibson Square Ventilation Shaft, an elegant disguise of ventilation for the Victoria Underground Line; the New Common Room Buildings, Gray's Inn; and the restoration of St Mary's Church, Paddington. He received two scholarships; one in Rome, the other from the Royal Academy in 1973 to study unreinforced domes, which took him to Italy and the Middle East. Following Erith's death in 1973, he continued in the same tradition of 'undiluted Classicism'.

'Modern architecture is a failure. I've always thought it didn't work, for structural and constructional reasons. It is only meant to last tens of years, not hundreds of years. It doesn't look very nice. And Classical buildings are no more expensive to build.

'The problem is not finding good craftmen these days, they're plentiful (well, at least they are in East Anglia). The problem is finding good patrons.'

Terry's clients include Alistair and David McAlpine; Anne Heseltine, wife of the Defence Secretary for whom he designed a summer house; and recently the large property company, Haselmere Estates, for

Common Room building and offices (centre) at Gray's Inn, London, 1971, by Quinlan Terry.

whom he designed Sandringham Court, a 7-storey office block and 25 flats in Soho, London. This is built of load-bearing brick – extremely rare at this height these days – and has classical detailing. It is very popular with the public and all the flats were sold (at 1984 prices from £60,000 for a studio to £95,000 for a two-bedroom flat) without even being advertised.

In 1985, the Department of the Environment and the Royal Fine Art Commission approved his £20-million redevelopment scheme beside the Thames at Richmond, previously approved by the local council, and which was favoured by a majority of five to one over alternatives in a public poll.

Waverton House, Moreton in Marsh, Gloucestershire, 1979, by Quinlan Terry.

The assumption that the specialists know better drags theory and practice into the bog of reactionary cosmopolitan opinion. The proletariat acquired the right to have their Corinthian colonnades.
JOSEPH STALIN

Pat Tindale
Chief Architect, Department of the Environment, London

Architecture is too important to be left to architects alone. Like crime, it is a problem for society as a whole.
BERTHOLD LUBETKIN
RIBA President's invitation lecture (1985)

In the two short centuries since architecture has become a well-defined profession of its own, its identity has afforded endless controversy. Is it an art practised by and for the sake of individuals, or a commercial enterprise geared to the needs of the market and the generation of profit, or a communal undertaking dedicated to the service of society?

Most enquirers rash enough to essay a serious answer to these questions have ended in admitting compromise – each or some of these ideas have a place in the best architecture. Architecture, if it is to go beyond the drawings board, is divided from the disciplines with which it is most often compared, the other 'arts', by the need to compromise, by the insistent demands of what is real and what is practical. Before these obligations all transcendent principles of 'truth' in architecture will always fall down. A compromise of ideals lies at the heart of the matter, to the chagrin of the pure in soul.
ANDREW SAINT
The Image of the Architect (1983)

Pat Tindale is an architect devoted to the public service. On leaving the Architectural Association school of architecture in 1948, she made a conscious decision that this was what she wanted to do, 'as I felt the public sector worked for the good of the community, the private sector for itself, although I soon discovered that was rather naive'. She went into schools first, then housing, for the Ministry of Housing Research and Development Group. Later she joined the Department of the Environment, where she was head of the Building Regulations Professional Division in 1972–4, Director of the Housing Development Directorate 1974–81, and Chief Architect from 1982.

'The system is scrupulously fair; there is no discrimination of any kind,' she says when questioned about the progress of her career. But she is used to taking tough decisions, and there are more and more which need to be made: 'Things were easier when everything was booming. And sometimes professional advice has to be tempered by political considerations.'

As Chief Architect, she is responsible for various groups working on Building Regulations, historic buildings, housing, regional affairs and the general promotion of architectural quality. Her department sponsors research to encourage developers to introduce art into their buildings. 'We identify particular opportunities and then take initiatives. I want to encourage the public to be more discriminating and to take a positive interest in the environment.

'Architects are a lively, imaginative bunch of people,' she says even though they have been 'battered and bemused' in recent times. The main problem facing architects, she believes, is adjusting to the severe reduction in workload of over the ten years to 1985. Conditions have changed from boom to recession.

'Architects have a more competitive, diversified role. There are community architects acting as entrepreneurs; multi-disciplinary teams; specialists in telecommunications and the new technologies. Clients are becoming more discriminating, but builders cannot be relied upon to build quality – a result of more self-employed building labour. At the same time, we need to make better use of our enormous building stock, while recognising the contribution that new buildings can make to the efficiency and profitability of an enterprise.'

PICTURE CREDITS

We would like to thank the following individuals and companies for allowing us to reproduce their copyright drawings and photographs.

62	Photri, Alexandria, Virginia
70	©ESTO, Mamaroneck, N.Y. (photo. Wolfgang Hoyt)
71 above	Reproduced with the permission of the Architectural Press, London
71 below	Wayne Andrews, Chicago
72	©ESTO, Mamaroneck, N.Y. (photo. Ezra Stoller)
73	©ESTO, Mamaroneck, N.Y. (photo. Ezra Stoller)
74	©Reading, London (Charles Knevitt Collection, London)
75	©Peter Brookes, London (Charles Knevitt Collection, London)
76	Photri, Alexandria, Virginia
77	Peter Vanderwarder, West Newton, Mass.
78	John Burgee Architects, with Philip Johnson, New York (photo. ©Richard Payne 1984)
79	Charles Knevitt, London
80	*Building Design,* London
81 left	*Building Design,* London
81 right	*Building Design,* London
82	Camera Press, London
84	Mary Evans Picture Library, London
85	GLC Photograph Library, London
86	GLC Photograph Library, London
87 above	The Mansell Collection, London
87 below	BBC Hulton Picture Library, London
88	Anglia Television, Norwich (photo. Philip King)
89	London Transport Photograph Library, London
90	Town and Country Planning Association, London
91 above	John Bethell, St Albans
91 below	*Oxford Mail and Times,* Oxford
92 left	Le Corbusier *Complète Oeuvre,* ©DACS 1985
92 right	Bettmann Archive, Inc., New York
94	Lucien Hervé, Paris
95 above	Reproduced with the permission of the Architectural Press, London
95 below	A. F. Kersting, London
97	*Yorkshire Post,* Leeds
98	Reproduced with the permission of the Architectural Press, London
99	Reproduced with the permission of the Architectural Press, London
101	Photo Source Ltd, London
102	Aerofilms Ltd., Elstree
103	Reproduced with the permission of the Architectural Press, London
104 above	Anglia Television, Norwich (photo. Philip King)
104 below	Anglia Television, Norwich (photo. Philip King)
105	Martin Charles, London
106	Reproduced with the permission of the Architectural Press, London
107 above	Reproduced with the permission of the Architectural Press, London
107 below	*Liverpool Daily Post and Echo,* Liverpool
108	Granada Publishing Ltd, London
109	Photo Source Ltd, London
110	UPI/Bettmann Newsphotos, New York
111	Reproduced with the permission of the Architectural Press, London
112	Associated Newspapers, London
113 top	Newcastle City Library, Local Studies Dept.
113 below	City of Newcastle, City Engineers Dept.
115	Barratt Developments Ltd, Newcastle-upon-Tyne
116	John Donat, London
118	Times Newspapers Ltd, London
118 inset	British Rail, Architect's Office, London
120	*Private Eye,* London
122	Camera Press, London (photo. Colin Davey)
123	Times Newspapers Ltd, London
124	John Donat, London
125	John Donat, London
126	Terry Farrell Partnership, London
127	John Donat, London
128	Times Newspapers Ltd, London
129	Lawrence Halprin and Associates, San Francisco
130	Wayne Andrews, Chicago
131	Arcaid Picture Library, London (photo. Richard Bryant)
132 left	Hunt Thompson Associates, London (photo. Martin Charles)
132 right	Hunt Thompson Associates, London (photo. Martin Charles)
133	Michael Twigg, Brown and Partners, London (drawn by A. Timothy)
134	*Liverpool Daily Post and Echo,* Liverpool (photo. Howard Davies)
135 above	Eric de Maré, Cirencester

135 below	*Liverpool Daily Post and Echo,* Liverpool (photo. Howard Davies)
136	BBC Hulton Picture Library, London
138 above	*Derby Evening Telegraph,* Derby
138	British Rail, Architect's Office, London
139	Urbed, London
141	Bradford Economic Development Unit, City of Bradford Metropolitan Council
142	John Donat, London
144	Eric de Maré, Cirencester
145	John Donat, London
146	Robert Howard, London
149	British Film Institute, London
150	Buckminster Fuller Institute, Los Angeles
152	©Magnum Photos Inc., London (photo. Dennis Stock)
156	D. Y. Davies and Associates, London
157	©The Open University Press 1985. *Energy Matters* booklet *Warm and Wise*
159	Centre for Alternative Technology, Machynlleth
160	Centre for Alternative Technology, Machynlleth
162	Bryan Avery, London
163	University of Minnesota. BRW Architects (photo. Philip MacMillan James)
164	University of Minnesota. BRW Architects (photo. Philip MacMillan James)
167	University of Minnesota. BRW Architects (photo. George Heindrich)
168 above	Reproduced with the permission of the Architectural Press, London
168 below	Anglia Television, Norwich (photo. Bob Hobbs)
169 left	Ahrends Burton and Koralek, London (photo. John Donat)
169 right	Times Newspapers Ltd, London
171 above	Charles Knevitt, London
171 below	©Louis Hellman, London (Charles Knevitt Collection, London)
173	Charles Knevitt, London
174	Hunt Thompson Associates, London
175	Peter Addis, London
177	Martin Charles, London
178	©Barry Fantoni, London (Charles Knevitt Collection, London)
181 above	©Louis Hellman, London (Charles Knevitt Collection, London)
181 below	©Louis Hellman, London
184	Robert Adam and Gebler Associates, Winchester
185 above	Robert Adam and Gebler Associates, Winchester
185 below	Ahrends Burton and Koralek, London (photo. John Donat)
186 left	Ahrends Burton and Koralek, London (photo. John Donat)
186 right	Ahrends Burton and Koralek, London (photo. John Donat)
188	Charles Knevitt, London
190	Martin Charles, London
191	Times Newspapers Ltd, London
192	Martin Charles, London
193	Arup Associates, Architects + Engineers + Quantity Surveyors, London
194	Terry Farrell Partnership, London
195 above	Foster Associates, London (photo Richard Davies)
195 below	Foster Associates, London (photo Richard Davies)
197	Barry Gasson, Glasgow
198	Skidmore, Owings and Merrill, Chicago
201	Murphy Jaan Architects, Chicago (photo. Keith Palmer, James Steinkamp)
202	Charles Knevitt, London
203	©Louis Hellman, London
204	Andrew Ward, London
205	Anglia Television, Norwich
207	Anglia Television, Norwich (photo. Iain Coates)
208 above	Times Newspapers Ltd, London
208 below	Building Design Partnership, London
210	Reproduced with the permission of the Architectural Press, London
211 above	©Hampshire County Architects Department
211 below	James Stirling, Michael Wilford and Associates, London
212 above	Anglia Television, Norwich (photo. Bob Hobbs)
212 below	Anglia Television, Norwich (photo. Bob Hobbs)
213 above	Times Newspapers Ltd, London
213 below	Erith and Terry Architects, Colchester
214	Charles Hall, Wormingford

Picture Research by Deborah Pownall.

BIBLIOGRAPHY
AND SUGGESTIONS FOR FURTHER READING

Architecture At The Threshold *(Introduction)*

BLAKE, PETER, *Form Follows Fiasco: Why Modern Architecture Hasn't Worked,* Boston and Toronto, Atlantic/Little, Brown, 1977.

CROSBY, THEO, *How to Play the Environment Game,* Harmondsworth, Arts Council of Great Britain and Penguin, 1973.

CURTIS, WILLIAM, J. R., *Modern Architecture since 1900,* Oxford, Phaidon, 1982.

DREXLER, ARTHUR, *Transformations in Modern Architecture,* Museum of Modern Art, New York, 1979.

ESHER, LIONEL, *A Broken Wave: The Rebuilding of England 1940–1980,* London, Allen Lane/Penguin, 1981.

HUGHES, ROBERT, *The Shock of the New,* London, BBC, 1980.

JENCKS, CHARLES and CHAITKIN, WILLIAM, *Current Architecture,* London, Academy Editions, 1982. Published in the U.S.A. as *Architecture Today.*

JENCKS, CHARLES, *Modern Movements in Architecture,* Harmondsworth, Penguin. First published 1973, Second Edition, 1985.

RAVETZ, ALISON, *Remaking Cities,* London, Croom Helm, 1980.

VENTURI, ROBERT, *Complexity and Contradiction in Architecture,* Museum of Modern Art, New York, 1966. Second Edition, London, Architectural Press, 1977.

WOLFE, TOM, *From Bauhaus to Our House,* London, Jonathan Cape, 1982.

One: 'A Nice Place to Be' *(Cities)*

BACON, EDMUND N., *Design of Cities,* London, Thames and Hudson. Revised Edition, 1975. First published 1967.

BURKE, GERALD, *Townscapes,* London, Pelican/Penguin, 1976.

CULLEN, GORDON, *The Concise Townscape,* London, Architectural Press, Paperback Edition, 1971. First published in hardback (unabridged) 1961.

GOSLING, DAVID and MAITLAND, BARRY, *Concepts of Urban Design,* London, Academy Editions, 1984.

JACOBS, JANE, *The Death and Life of Great American Cities,* Harmondsworth, Pelican/Penguin, 1965; re-issued 1972. First published in the U.S.A. by Random House 1961. Published in Great Britain by Jonathan Cape, 1962.

JENSEN, ROBERT and CONWAY, PATRICIA, *Ornamentalism: The New Decorativeness in Architecture and Design,* London, Allen Lane/Penguin, 1983. Originally published in the U.S.A. by Clarkson N. Potter, Inc., 1982.

LYNCH, KEVIN, *The Image of the City,* Cambridge, Massachusetts and London, MIT Press, 1960.

MUMFORD, LEWIS, *The City in History,* Harmondsworth, Pelican/Penguin, 1966. First published in the U.S.A. 1961. Published by Secker & Warburg, 1961.

RABAN, JONATHAN, *Soft City,* London, Fontana/Collins, 1975. First published by Hamish Hamilton, 1974.

RUDOFSKY, BERNARD, *Streets for People: A Primer for Americans,* Garden City, New York, Anchor Press/Doubleday, 1969.

TOWNSEND, PETER (EDITOR), *Art Within Reach,* 'Art Monthly' in collaboration with the Arts Council of Great Britain and the Crafts Council, Thames and Hudson, 1984.

Two: Cathedrals of Commerce *(Skyscrapers)*

ATTOE, WAYNE, *Skylines: Understanding and Molding Urban Silhouettes,* Chichester, John Wiley & Sons, 1981.

BACH, IRA J., *Chicago's Famous Buildings,* Chicago and London, University of Chicago Press, Third Edition, 1980. First published 1965; Second Edition 1969.

BANHAM, REYNER, *The Architecture of the Well-tempered Environment,* London/Chicago, Architectural Press/University of Chicago Press, 1969.

GAVOIS, JEAN, *Going Up: An Informal History of the Elevator from the Pyramids to the Present,* London, Otis Elevator Company, 1983.

GOLDBERGER, PAUL, *New York: The City Observed,* Harmondsworth, Penguin, 1982.

GOLDBERGER, PAUL, *The Skyscraper,* London, Allen Lane/Penguin, 1982.

JENCKS, CHARLES, *Skyscrapers – Skycities,* London, Academy Editions, 1980.

KOOLHAAS, REM, *Delirious New York,* London, Academy Editions, 1978.

SHARP, DENNIS (EDITOR), *Alfred C. Bossom's American Architecture 1903– 1926,* London, Book Art, 1984.

WHITE, NORVAL and WILLENSKY, ELLIOT, *AIA Guide to New York City,* New York, Collier Books, London, Collier Macmillan, Revised Edition, 1978.

YEE, ROGER and GUSTAFSON, KAREN, *Corporate Design: The Interior Design and Architecture of Corporate America,* London, Thames and Hudson, 1983. First published in the U.S.A., New York, Interior Design Books, a division of Whitney Communications Corporation, 1983.

Three: Home, Sweet Consumer Durable *(Housing)*

BELL, COLIN and ROSE, *City Fathers: The Early History of Town Planning in Britain,* Harmondsworth, Pelican/Penguin, 1972. First published by Barrie & Rockliff, The Cresset Press, 1967.

COLEMAN, ALICE, *Utopia on Trial: Vision and Reality in Planned Housing,* London, Hilary Shipman, 1985.

DARLEY, GILLIAN, *Villages of Vision,* St Alban's, Granada/Paladin, 1978. First published by the Architectural Press, 1975.

DUNLEAVY, PATRICK, *The Politics of Mass Housing in Britain, 1945–1975,* Oxford, Clarendon Press, 1981. Published in the U.S.A. by Oxford University Press, New York.

GREATER LONDON COUNCIL, *Home Sweet Home: Housing designed by the LCC and GLC Architects 1888–1975,* London, Academy Editions, 1976.

PAWLEY, MARTIN, *Architecture versus Housing,* London, Studio Vista, 1971. Published in the U.S.A. by Praeger Publishers, New York and Washington.

RUSSELL, BARRY, *Building Systems, Industrialization and Architecture,* London, John Wiley & Sons, 1981.

TAYLOR, NICHOLAS, *The Village in the City,* London, Temple Smith, 1973. Published in association with New Society.

Four: A Future For The Past *(Conservation)*

BINNEY, MARCUS, *Our Vanishing Heritage,* London, Arlington Books, 1984.

CANTACUZINO, SHERBAN and BRANDT, SUSAN, *Saving Old Buildings,* London, Architectural Press, 1980.

ESHER, LIONEL, *The Continuing Heritage: The Story of the Civic Trust Awards,* London, Franey, 1982.

INSALL, DONALD and DEPARTMENT OF THE ENVIRONMENT, DIRECTORATE OF ANCIENT MONUMENTS AND HISTORIC BUILDINGS, *Conservation in Action: Chester's Bridgegate,* London, HMSO, 1982.

LLOYD, DAVID W., *The Making of English Towns: 2000 Years of Evolution,* London, Victor Gollancz in association with Peter Crawley, 1984.

LOWENTHAL, DAVID and BINNEY, MARCUS (EDITORS), *Our Past Before Us: Why Do We Save It?,* London, Temple Smith, 1981.

LYNCH, KEVIN, *What Time is This Place?* Cambridge, Massachusetts and London, MIT Press, Paperback Edition, 1976.

Five: New Directions *(Future Developments)*

HALL, PETER (EDITOR), *Europe 2000,* London, Duckworth, 1977.

HATCH, RICHARD, C. (EDITOR), *The Scope of Social Architecture,* New York, Van Nostrand Reinhold, 1984.

ILLICH, IVAN, ET AL. *Disabling Professions,* London, Marion Boyars, 1977.

ILLICH, IVAN, *Tools for Conviviality,* London, Calder & Boyars, 1973. Published in the U.S.A. by Harper and Row, New York.

JENCKS, CHARLES, *Architecture 2000: Predictions and Methods,* London, Studio Vista, 1971.

KNEVITT, CHARLES and WATES, NICK, *Community Architecture: How people can shape their own Environment,* Harmondsworth, Penguin, 1986.

SCHUMACHER, E. F., *Small is Beautiful: A Study of Economics as if People Mattered,* London, Abacus/Sphere Books, 1974. First published by Blond & Briggs, London, 1973.

SHECKLEY, ROBERT, *Futuropolis,* London, Bergström and Boyle, Big O Publishing, 1979.

TOFFLER, ALVIN, *Previews and Premises,* London, Pan, 1984.

TOFFLER, ALVIN, *The Third Wave,* London, Collins, 1980; Pan Books, 1981. Published in the U.S.A. by Morrow, 1980 and Bantam, 1981.

WARD, COLIN, *Tenants Take Over,* London, Architectural Press, 1974.

WARD, COLIN, *Utopia,* Harmondsworth, Penguin Education, 1974.

WARD, COLIN, *When We Build Again: Let's have Housing that Works!,* London and Leichhardt, Australia, Pluto Press, 1985.

WOLF, PETER, *The Future of the City: New Directions in Urban Planning,* New York, Whitney Library of Design, 1974.

Six: The Architects *(General)*

COOK, JOHN W. and KLOTZ, HEINRICH, *Conversations with Architects,* London, Lund Humphries Publishers, 1973. Published in the U.S.A. by Praeger Publishers Inc., New York.

JENCKS, CHARLES, *Late Modern Architecture,* London, Academy Editions, 1980.

JENCKS, CHARLES, *The Language of Post-Modern Architecture,* London, Academy Editions, Fourth Edition, 1984.

LASDUN, DENYS (EDITOR), *Architecture in an Age of Scepticism,* London, Heinemann, 1984.

PAPADAKIS, ANDREAS C. (EDITOR), *British Architecture,* London, Architectural Design and AD Editions, 1982; 1984. Published in the U.S.A. by St Martin's Press, New York.

SAINT, ANDREW, *The Image of the Architect,* New Haven and London, Yale University Press, 1983.

Individual Architects

Arup Associates: BRAWNE, MICHAEL, *Arup Associates: The Biography of an Architectural Practice,* London, Lund Humphries Publishers, 1983.

Cullinan, Edward: *Edward Cullinan Architects,* London, RIBA Publications, 1984.

Erskine, Ralph: *Ralph Erskine,* London, Architectural Design, Vol. 47, No. 11–12, 1977.

Farrell, Terry: *Terry Farrell,* London and New York, Academy Editions/St Martin's Press, 1984.

Foster, Norman: *Foster Associates,* London, RIBA Publications, 1979. *Norman Foster, Architect: Selected Works 1962–84,* ALISTAIR BEST, Whitworth Art Gallery, Manchester, Exhibition Catalogue, 1984.

Foster Associates: Six Architectural Projects 1975–1985, Sainsbury Centre for the Visual Arts, University of East Anglia, Norwich, Exhibition Catalogue, 1985.

Johnson, Philip: *Johnson/Burgee: Architecture,* NORY MILLER, New York, Random House, 1979.

Lasdun, Denys: *A Language and a Theme: The Architecture of Denys Lasdun & Partners,* London, RIBA Publications, 1976.

Portman, John: *The Architect as Developer,* JOHN PORTMAN and JONATHAN BARNETT, New York, McGraw Hill, 1976.

Rogers, Richard: *Lloyd's of London,* London, Edizioni Tecno, 1985.

Richard Rogers & Architects, London, Academy Editions/St Martin's Press, 1985.

Skidmore, Owings & Merrill: *SOM: Architecture and Urbanism 1973-83,* Stuttgart, Verlag Gerd Hatje/Van Nostrand Reinhold, 1983.

Stirling, James: *James Stirling,* London, RIBA Drawings Collection Catalogue, RIBA Publications, 1974, Second Edition 1976.

James Stirling: Buildings and Projects, London, Architectural Press, 1984.

Terry, Quinlan: *Quinlan Terry,* London, Architectural Design/Academy Editions, 1981.

INDEX

QUOTATIONS

GENERAL INDEX

References in italic refer to illustrations and/or captions. Major entries (particularly the architects' biographies) are in bold.